MARK IPPOLI
206. 605. 2911
M.E.M.C.

M000289053

Additional Praise for *The Co-Creation Edge*

"Commercial insurers, like many other industries, have to learn to co-create not only with their customers, but also with their distributors, intermediaries, and trading partners. Gouillart and Quancard provide the best framework I have seen on how to build those customer ecosystems and provide an engagement model to encourage co-creation and better utilization of shared data."

—Peter Linn, CEO North America, AXA MATRIX Risk Consultants

"As the business environment is changing, strategic account management becomes a key to success. The book by Gouillart and Quancard provides a roadmap for all sales people wanting to survive and grow."

—Corrado Cesti, Head of Heavy Industry, SKF

"In healthcare, the need to manage outcome data is transforming account management as we know it. The *Co-Creation Edge* will show you the process through which a few pioneers engage new communities of players, utilize novel data platforms and hence accelerate the journey towards significantly improved patient outcomes, benefiting all stakeholders involved."

—Huw Tippett, Global Head Customer Excellence, Baxalta

Francis Gouillart • Bernard Quancard

The Co-Creation Edge

Harnessing Big Data to Transform Sales and Procurement for Business Innovation

Francis Gouillart
Concord, Massachusetts, USA

Bernard Quancard
Chicago, Illinois, USA

ISBN 978-1-137-52675-5   ISBN 978-1-137-52677-9   (eBook)
DOI 10.1057/978-1-137-52677-9

Library of Congress Control Number: 2016906964

Cover illustration: © Dorling Kindersley/Thinkstock

Printed on acid-free paper

This Palgrave Macmillan imprint is published by Springer Nature
The registered company is Nature America Inc. New York

Contents

Figures

CHAPTER 1

The Changing World of Sales and Procurement

Let us start with the bad news. Thousands of sales and procurement people are threatened with extinction.

If you're a sales person solely relying on your interpersonal skills to gain access to customers, your knowledge of the company's products and your negotiation ability, you may be in trouble. Here is how you will know. Are you experiencing any of the following symptoms?

- You're no longer dealing with individual decision-makers with unique needs and the latitude to call their own shots.
- The central procurement people you are required to work with have standardized the buying process, and they have little time, or inclination, to meet with you, except for quarterly business reviews where they challenge you on service incidents and price.
- Purchasing uses reverse auctions to get the lowest price.
- Your technical colleagues at the company complain that you're not selling the latest solutions and wonder aloud "whether you're getting where the company's going".
- Sales quotas rise every year while your company's product differentiation erodes. Your status is diminished; your bonus shrinks or disappears, and your salary gets frozen.
- The sales function gets periodically reorganized, leading you to wonder after each reorganization whether you still have a job.

Like air running out of a balloon, the fun of being in sales is slowly and steadily disappearing.

The situation isn't much better if you're a purchasing person. For a while, procurement departments were riding high, but most of the gains from vendor consolidation have been reaped and you struggle to keep adding value. Reflect on whether you're experiencing any of the following:

- Your traditional skills of knowing your category, managing rigorous Request for Proposal (RFP) processes, and negotiating hard with suppliers don't seem to cut it anymore.
- New automated tools create supplier transparency more effectively than pressing suppliers for that information in live interviews.
- As waves of corporate cost reductions hit, you're being asked to handle more and more categories, leaving you with less and less time to familiarize yourself with each of them.
- You run from meeting to meeting and the day gets increasingly longer.
- You're being exhorted by your technical people to extract more value from your suppliers, and demand innovation from them, but you're not sure exactly what that means.
- Suppliers continually attempt to end-run you by going directly to technical people inside your company and your role is threatened.

At night, you start wondering whether procurement is the career you thought it was going to be. It all feels pretty bleak in procurement land.

For sales and procurement alike, it does not have to be that way. Here is the good news.

Sales and procurement professionals have a bright future ahead of them if they can respond to six trends we observe in the business-to-business world. Each trend offers an opportunity to develop a new skill for sales and procurement professionals and adopt a new practice. Because these practices are not yet widely adopted as "best practices", we refer to them as "next practices", i.e., they are likely to become best practices over time, but they can only be found in the most innovative companies. Each of them offers an opportunity for sales and procurement professionals to add new value.

Here are the six trends and corresponding next practices.

1   Trend #1: The Problems that Companies' Sales and Procurement People Are Asked to Tackle Are Broader and More Complex Than Ever

Next Practice #1: Sales and Procurement Professionals Work Together to Address New Problems of Increasing Magnitude

The scope of problems tackled by the best sales and procurement people is dramatically increasing. Yes, sales and procurement's bread and butter is still to reduce cost or improve operations. But sales and procurement professionals are becoming more and involved in helping their companies develop new products. Some of them are tackling issues that extend beyond the supplier and the customer firm and drive the transformation of other companies upstream or downstream of them. Frequently, sales and procurement even go beyond that. It used to be that business focused on making money for investors, while government and non-profit entities worried about solving societal or quality-of-life, human issues. Today, this distinction has become blurred, and companies are playing a leading role in grappling with large social, environmental or economic problems, and sales and procurement often lead the charge.

Look at the scope of problems tackled by successful companies. These are vast, demanding problems requiring the orchestration of a complex ecosystem of players, thereby redefining the role of both sales and procurement. IBM sells products and services that enable what the firm calls "a Smarter Planet", linking together public and private players to optimize traffic flow or energy consumption of entire cities.[1] Unilever's procurement is responsible for transforming the agriculture-to-food value chain of produce, such as tomatoes, toward greater sustainability.[2] Schneider Electric sells energy efficiency across a complex chain of technical intermediaries, distributors and end-users.[3] The Medical-Surgical Division of Becton Dickinson (BD) sells the idea that it can

[1] A description of the IBM Smarter Planet vision is provided at http://www.ibm.com/smarterplanet/us/en/. For a video describing the concept by Ginni Rometty, CEO of IBM, see her Singapore 2013 speech at https://www.youtube.com/watch?v=iNZj38sD81w.
[2] For an understanding of Unilever's sustainability strategy, see https://www.unilever.com/sustainable-living/the-sustainable-living-plan/our-strategy/. For a description of Unilever's specific practices for tomatoes, see https://www.unilever.com/Images/2004-sustainable-tomatoes-good-agricultural-practice-guidelines_tcm244-424300_1.pdf.
[3] See for example Overview of the Group's Strategy, Markets and Businesses, published in 2014, available at http://www2.schneider-electric.com/documents/sustainable-development/sustainability-investors-analysts/schneider-electric-overview-of-core-business.pdf.

reduce hospital-acquired infections across a complex chain of independent doctors, large hospitals, city managers and health regulators.[4] The sale of GE's Ecomagination products explicitly tackle the environment as a core issue.[5] Problems don't get much bigger than that, and sales and procurement people at those companies can orchestrate the complex problem-solving required to convert those solutions into revenues or purchases.

This trend of companies tackling large societal issues is even more apparent in emerging countries such as Brazil, India or China, where problems of poverty, health or infrastructure development are of such scale and urgency that they demand the mobilization of business to solve them, leading the sales and procurement people at Indian companies like Tata[6] or Infosys[7] to constantly promote, or demand, "triple bottom-line" accountability (triple bottom-line measurement involves measuring economic, social and sustainability outcomes). Another company, ITC of India,[8] wants to transform agriculture as we know it by procuring products with a richer social and lesser environmental footprint. Because sales and procurement people sit at the edge of their firms, they are in the best position to connect the agenda of both firms (supplier and customer) and mobilize them to solve those irking societal issues.

[4] Becton Dickinson's (BD) co-creation strategy toward hospitals' Independent Doctors Network is described in a Harvard Business Review article entitled *Community-Powered Problem-Solving*, written by Francis Gouillart and Douglas Billings, April 2013. The emergence of the original idea behind the strategy is described in more detail in Chap. 4 of this book.

[5] See http://www.ge.com/about-us/ecomagination for a discussion of GE's Ecomagination approach.

[6] See for example People, Planet, Prosperity section of Tata Steel's website, available at: http://www.tatasteeleurope.com/en/sustainability/sustainability-challenges/people-planet-prosperity.

[7] See Forbes article entitled Sustainability: What You Cannot Measure, You Cannot Manage, October 2011, by Dipak Rath, available at http://www.forbes.com/sites/infosys/2011/10/10/sustainability-measurement/.

[8] The multi-stakeholder aspect of ITC Agribusiness' strategy is particularly visible through its e-choupal initiative. See ITC e-choupal web site for a description of the approach, at http://www.itcportal.com/businesses/agri-business/e-choupal.aspx. The e-choupal initiative is also described in the book The Power of Co-Creation, written by Venkat Ramaswamy and Francis Gouillart, Free Press, 2010.

2   *Trend #2: Sales and Procurement Networks Are Becoming More Diffuse and Complex*

Next Practice #2: Sales and Procurement Professionals Organize Problem-Solving Networks Across Company Boundaries

We used to think of sales and procurement as one-on-one, hard-nosed negotiations. Today, B2B sales or sourcing professionals have to weave together a complex network of players on the side of at least two companies (supplier and customer), often more when suppliers of the supplier, or customers of the customer, are included. Inside each company, the selling and procurement managers need to mobilize a large number of operational and technical people. This requires a careful orchestration of interactions by the lead sales and procurement people, a patient weaving together of a network of individuals across multiple entities and geographies to address issues of common interest. Today, successful sales and procurement people have to become masters at organizing problem-solving communities across supplier and customer firms (and often beyond). The skill set required is the ability to engage distant people in solving problems together, a task vastly different from conducting heroic negotiations.

Think of what a large account manager has to do if she is part of Hewlett Packard Enterprise (HPE)[9] and responsible for the sales of her firm to a large retailer such as Walmart.[10] On the HPE sales side, she has to worry about coordinating her efforts with her account manager colleagues in the Services division (responsible for service sales) and the account manager for HPE's Consulting Group (responsible for consulting sales). She needs to work with field service engineers located in Walmart stores and at headquarters, and the HPE call centers who handle problems at three levels of resolution called L1, L2 and L3. On the marketing and product front, if the negotiation involves any kind of new offering, which would typically be the case for such a large a client as Walmart, she needs to work with the portfolio managers of HPE's Products, Services and Consulting divisions.

[9] For an introduction to the history and competitive position of HP, see for example the vendor profile provided by Enterprise Network Planet at http://www.enterprisenetworkingplanet.com/HP/.
[10] For a description of Walmart IT needs, see October 2014 release by the company at http://corporate.walmart.com/_news_/news-archive/2014/10/15/walmart-will-accelerate-investments-in-e-commerce-and-moderate-global-square-footage-growth.

On the technical front, and, given the innovative content of any new negotiation between the two firms, she has to involve the HPE CTO, as well as the R&D groups for hardware and software development. And that's just HPE negotiating with itself so far.

On the Walmart side, our SAM deals, directly or indirectly, with the senior buyer on price and term issues, with the CTO on IT strategy and network issues, with the Network department of the IT division on numerous operational issues, with the IT people in the individual Walmart stores, with the business users of specific applications (say, sales function within Walmart for a point-of-sales system problem) and with numerous third parties, such as application developers, resellers, network service shops and consultants to Walmart.

3   Trend #3: People Expect Problems to Be Solved in Real Time as a Group

Next Practice #3: Sales and Procurement Professionals Must Structure a Process and Platform for Live Cross-Company Engagement

Today, everything happens in real time. Solving problems requires getting together in physical meetings, or by phone, video-conferencing or web-conferencing, using whatever data is available to make the case for the joint engagement. Sales and procurement professionals are now the initiators and facilitators of this engagement process; their role is to orchestrate the flow of problem-solving meetings and share common information across company boundaries to get things going. As in old times, they still set up meetings, but these are no longer one-on-one "sales meetings" in the traditional sense where a "suspect" is transformed into a "prospect" and eventually into a "sale" by "overcoming objections".

These new meetings take the form of problem-solving workshops involving multiple stakeholders where people agree to launch exploratory initiatives that will be proved, or disproved, through observable data. The role of sales and procurement is to initiate, nurture and grow the engagement and to provide the process and platforms required, with the actual problem solving done by others. Insights resulting into sales are not generated by blinding flashes of brilliance by sales people; they come from the painstaking process of multiple players at the supplier and customer levels working together with flip charts and markers and making proprietary company data transparent to each other.

Capgemini, the global IT services firm headquartered in France,[11] is representative of the trend toward using live, group-based problem-solving platforms to tackle urgent corporate issues and accelerate the sale or procurement of a solution. Capgemini has developed a structured, workshop-based process of engagement called Accelerated Solution Environment (ASE) that it effectively uses as part of its relationship-building process with its major clients and prospects. The firm offers this service in various parts of the world, providing a combination of physical space (modular, creativity-friendly layout with heavy reliance on visual representations) and human talent trained in the facilitation of groups (ASE facilitators are a dedicated group). The workshop is viewed as the culmination point of a rigorous process lasting a few weeks, where sponsors are coached into paying close attention to the definition of the problem and inviting the right people to the workshop, such that a solution can be developed in real time with all the relevant parties accountable for the implementation of the solution.

4   Trend #4: Big Data Has Arrived in Sales and Procurement

Next Practice #4: Sales and Procurement Facilitate the Development of New Data-Driven, Cross-Company Interactions Fed by Digital Platforms

Today, data permeates all aspects of selling and buying. Quarterly business reviews are full of numbers, from reviews of sales and spend to incident reports or forecasts. Much customer relationship management (CRM) and supplier relationship management (SRM) software has been purchased on both sides in the last few years on the assumption that the data generated would generate new insights. The growth of such software notwithstanding, many sales and procurement professionals have experienced firsthand that generating meaningful opportunities from the data is far from a simple process.

The most advanced sales and procurement professionals convert the meeting process of the early engagement they have created, with its relatively informal exchange of information, into a more structured set of cross-company interactions with a measurable outcome. In other words, they design formal

---

[11] A description of Capgemini's Accelerated Solutions Environment (ASE), can be found on the company's website at https://www.capgemini-consulting.com/acceleration-capabilities/accelerated-solution-environments.

experiments between their company and the other party, create consensus on what outcomes both companies are trying to generate, and use the existing IT platforms of the firm to measure those outcomes. The idea is to prove that the solutions conceptualized early on in the relationship actually produce the envisioned results. Most of the time, some of this can be done with existing systems, but in many cases, this approach requires developing new interactions, or "apps", on the back of the existing system, and using new digital tools to connect the two companies. The ability to transition from qualitative meetings-driven engagement to hard-wired, data-driven interactions is a key skill of high-performing sales and procurement professionals. Over time, no collaborative sales or procurement program is sustainable without some kind of data feed and infrastructural IT platform to support it, since meetings alone rapidly become costly and cumbersome.

John Deere Construction[12] illustrates this approach where sales and procurement professionals develop structured interactions supported by data and an IT platform. Account managers at John Deere who call on large construction dealers and large construction companies and their procurement counterparts have a secret weapon called Worksight™ (it was previously known as JD Link®).[13] Each John Deere machine used on a construction site "beams" information back to headquarters about where the machine is located (which helps maximize machine utilization and prevent theft), how the machine is used by its operator (which allows coaching of the operator if the machine is left idle for too long or pushed too hard), or how worn out some of the machine parts are (which allows replacing parts before they break).

The Worksight™ platform allows the Deere account manager and his purchasing counterpart at the dealer or construction company to redefine their role: instead of being "metal pushers" on the sale side and "metal buyers" on the procurement side, both now have the opportunity to become central orchestrators of a network of operational people (from machine operators to foremen to maintenance people, energy analysts or equipment designers)

---

[12] For a basic description of John Deere Construction and Forestry division, see https://www.deere.com/en_US/industry/construction/john_deere_construction_forestry_division/john_deere_construction_and_forestry_division.page.

[13] In January 2015, John Deere Construction released a series of videos that explain how the Worksight™ system works. They are available at: https://www.deere.com/en_US/corporate/our_company/news_and_media/press_releases/2015/construction/2015jan14-worksight.page.

who discuss how they can reduce their total cost of operation by looking at the data.

This makes the role of the Deere account managers and procurement managers at the dealers and construction companies more strategic than before. The technology and the data are an indispensable ingredient of success, but the ability of the sales and procurement professionals to structure and facilitate the human network around the problem-solving interactions offered by the technology is what drives actual results. They can set up maintenance groups, energy consumption groups, operator learning groups, and even machine design groups where users give John Deere's engineers feedback on how to improve the machines themselves. Nobody is in a better place to initiate those problem-solving interactions through data than the sales people of the supplier and the procurement people of the customer. The reward for Deere sales people is to create loyalty with dealers and construction company customers, while procurement people at the dealer and construction companies are recognized for generating value beyond reducing the capital expenditure budget of their firm.

5   Trend #5: Sales and Procurement Professionals Use Their Own Transformation to Transform the Work Experience of Others

Next Practice # 5: Sales and Procurement Professionals Facilitate the Creation of New Personal Experiences for Individuals in Their Network

It has become a cliché to say that one has to personally transform before attempting to transform others. Yet, this is what the most innovative sales and procurement professionals do. The transformation of sales people from quota-driven, product-focused deal-makers to orchestrators of broad-based, problem-solving networks using data to generate revenue has been remarkable at many companies. Some procurement people have undergone a matching transformation, changing their focus from price- and service-level agreements to becoming facilitators of innovative supplier networks that generate value for their company way beyond reducing spend in the category they manage. For both sales and procurement people who have developed these new skills, the quality of their work experience has increased dramatically, because they have enjoyed success and its economic implications of better salaries, better bonuses and faster advancement.

In many cases, though, sales and procurement people have also enjoyed a subtler improvement in the quality of their personal experience of work: because of the adoption of broader social or environmental missions by many corporations, their business life has also become more meaningful, allowing a better cross-over to their personal life. Instead of treating work life solely as the provider of financial resources to be reinvested into more soulful personal activities, work life and personal life have become integrated, allowing people to feel better about their business experience.

The best sales and procurement professionals are able to trigger a matching transformation with the people they deal with. They create a wave of empathy around themselves and what they're doing, causing their counterparts to want to join in the problem-solving quest with them. Because personal experience is a viral thing, people inside the network of those sales and procurement professionals gradually want to join in, hoping to reach the same level of meaning in their work.

Ruben Taborda,[14] who was long Chief Purchasing Officer (CPO) of the Medical Devices and Diagnostics at Johnson and Johnson (J&J), offers a good example of personal transformation inducing the transformation of others. In addition to his duties as CPO for one of the three divisions of J&J, he was also in charge of the company's women- and minority-owned supplier program. Although there are many others, J&J's flagship program is the Billion Dollar Roundtable initiative.[15] The Billion Dollar Roundtable (BDR) is a club of 20 companies who, like J&J, buy more than one billion dollars from suppliers that are owned by women or minority people.

The BDR program has a lot of structural implications for J&J's Procurement organization. The company must tabulate in a scorecard what it buys from companies that qualify as women- and minority-owned businesses. It has to dedicate some procurement and human resources staff to foster the use of those minority suppliers by purchasing category managers who would otherwise not bother. The same staff has to coach women- and minority-owned suppliers who are often in early stages of development on how to deal with the sometimes intimidating sourcing processes of J&J.

---

[14] For background of Ruben Taborda, see Linkedin resume at: https://www.linkedin.com/pub/ruben-dario-taborda/5/943/647.
[15] A description of the Billion Dollar Roundtable can be found at: http://www.billiondollarroundtable.org/.

But what long drove the whole program is the larger-than-life personality of Taborda and the ability he has of mobilizing everybody around him about the need to transform the fate of women and minorities through procurement. His ability to create empathy is rooted in his own experience of life: he was born in a large Colombian family in Miami and was exposed early to the social challenges of minorities in the US, with its cohort of poverty and law enforcement issues. For a long time, he kept his own background and personal life separate from his professional life. After college, he went through various jobs in sales and procurement at J&J, until he was asked out of the blue by the CEO a few years ago to lead the women- and minority-owned program at J&J.

In his CPO job, Taborda's business and personal life became inextricably linked. One of his sisters is a cop and he started to view his role as CPO of one of J&J's businesses as instrumental in addressing the issues faced by his sister. He constantly asked himself the following question: how can we give opportunities for young Hispanics in Florida so that they do not end up being arrested by my sister? Taborda also lost one of his parents to diabetes at a fairly young age, was what he calls himself "a fat kid", and cannot help but view his own family as a test of whether J&J is accomplishing its mission to improve world health. Taborda developed a powerful vision that J&J can create an ecosystem of suppliers, employees and customers who can transform the health, economic and social fate of women and minorities in business.

One of his most intriguing ideas is that corporate purchasing mandates to consolidate suppliers makes it difficult for them to take advantage of innovation by smaller, entrepreneurial, socially creative firms. Ignoring these companies, or forcing them into premature consolidation inside larger groups, is counterproductive and, yet, what most large company procurement groups are incented to do.

Here is how he expressed it in one of our conversations: "At Johnson & Johnson, our commitment to Supplier Diversity is a representation of the third tenet of Our Credo, which speaks to our responsibility to the communities where we live and work. Partnering with diverse and small businesses creates jobs and builds wealth in the communities in which we operate. Increasingly, diversity and inclusion is something our customers are paying attention to, and we remain focused on ensuring that our supplier base reflects our patient, customer and employee base. As our business becomes more global, having a diverse supplier base strengthens our ability to conduct business across all cultures and geographies. We also believe these partnerships have the ability to generate innovations in health care that can lead to new products, services, and treatments for disease, innovations that will not only help us care for the world, one person at a time, but can help us change the world together".[16]

While fighting the dominant logic of supplier consolidation makes the task difficult, it is not impossible. In particular, it has proven difficult for many suppliers to resist Taborda when he talked to them across the table about what they had to do together, particularly given the purchasing fire power that he represented through his CPO role at J&J.

6   Trend #6: Sales and Procurement Professionals Are Asked to Constantly Reinvent the Business Model of Their Firms

Next Practice #6: Sales and Procurement Professionals Find New Sources of Value for Their Firm

It should be pretty clear, by now, that firms must constantly evolve their business model if they are to succeed. Competitive advantage is a fleeting thing; neither sales, nor procurement are allowed to rest on the laurels of their firm for too long. While some companies rely on mergers and acquisitions to create new sources of value, most companies transform more gradually, one contract at a time. Each sale or purchase becomes the blueprint for the next one, gradually changing the way the company sells or buys, until the original model "morphs" beyond recognition into a new model. Since sales and procurement professionals are the keepers of each new negotiation or contract, this gives them a privileged vantage point when it comes to finding new sources of value for both supplier and customer.

At Shell, the IT procurement function attached to the CIO is fundamentally changing the way it creates value for the firm.[17] Rather than pitting IT competitors against each other to drive down price and secure more services, as is traditionally the case, the company has been trying since 2008 to solve what it perceives as a fundamental problem: the fact that not enough IT

---

[16] Interview of Ruben Taborda by Francis Gouillart, October 2015.

[17] For a discussion of Shell's procurement strategy, see the interview of Alan Matula's CIO in the McKinsey Quarterly article entitled Managing IT transformation on a global scale, March 2010. It is available at http://www.mckinsey.com/insights/business_technology/managing_it_transformation_on_a_global_scale_an_interview_with_shell_cio_alan_matula.

R&D resources are directed toward B2B "enterprise computing" of the type needed by Shell, as a result of Silicon Valley's dominant focus on the consumer market.

To address the issue, Shell is trying to foster some redirecting of IT R&D resources toward more B2B IT research within a few major IT companies it has selected as its partners. These partners have been placed in specific categories such as foundation (e.g., Oracle, Microsoft, Cisco), infrastructure (e.g., AT&T or Hewlett Packard), or applications (e.g., Accenture or Wipro). The *quid pro quo* is the following: Shell protects those companies from the vicissitudes of continuous poaching in their category by other large partners it has selected, which encourages them to play nice with each other, not a natural trait of large IT competitors, but, in exchange, it asks them to assemble and manage a full ecosystem of smaller innovative suppliers whose capabilities are brought to Shell. The idea is to reconnect Shell's R&D with each supplier ecosystem's R&D, encourage more investment in technology areas of interest to Shell, and create new sources of competitive advantage for the firm through technology.

Now place yourself in the shoes of the traditional IT buyer at Shell and imagine the mutation of skills required to go from hard-nosed IT buyer to relationship manager for the IT supplier and the ecosystem of firms it has assembled. Extracting the new source of value for Shell changes everything in the life of the procurement professional, from whom he deals with, to what his engagement process needs to be, or what data he should look at. Similarly, visualize how different the role of the Shell strategic account managers at Cisco or Accenture has to be in order to implement Shell's vision of their firm working, not only as a traditional large supplier pushing sales, but also as a joint R&D partner, and as the federator of an ecosystem of smaller firms bringing innovative capabilities to Shell.

7   Implications for Strategic Account Managers and Senior Procurement Managers

The six trends we have outlined point to a stark choice for senior account managers and senior procurement managers alike. Either they adapt to the new reality of selling and procurement, or they will inexorably be replaced by web-based or channel-based alternatives that will do most of what they do today at a fraction of the cost. Increasingly, there is no middle ground

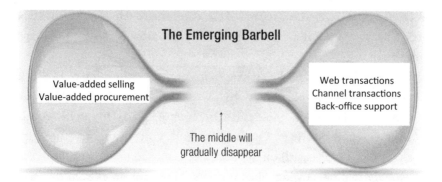

Fig. 1.1 Where sales and procurement are headed (*Source*: Strategic Account Management Association)

anymore. SAMs and senior buyers will either evolve into high value-added sales and procurement professionals, or disappear.

Figure 1.1 illustrates the choice that faces them.

So what do all these trends add up to? What are the implications for sales and procurement professionals of these large changes impacting their craft?

Putting together all the trends we have reviewed so far, we believe a new model of sales and procurement is emerging, which we call co-creation. This is the object of the next chapter.

CHAPTER 2

The Co-Creation Cycle

In Chap. 1, we saw the various trends at play at the intersection of suppliers and customers. Each of those trends poses a specific challenge for strategic account managers (SAMs) and procurement managers. In this section, we show how both parties need to come up with a new model of how to work together in the new environment. We call this model co-creation.

> *Co-creation is the cycle of engagement through which a strategic account manager and a senior procurement person agree to structure new interactions involving members of the supplier and customer communities beyond themselves, and through the use of data, transform the professional experience of all players, and ultimately produce new sources of value that supplier and customer can share.*

Admittedly, this is a mouthful, so let's break out this definition into its major components. Co-creation is a *cycle* involving identifiable phases we will outline in this chapter that get repeated over time. It is a cycle of *engagement* because it is about capturing the (emotional) hearts and (rational) minds of the individuals involved in the co-creation on both the supplier and customer sides. Some aspects of co-creation are left-brained and rational (the use of data to create insights), while other aspects are right-brained (emotional attraction of tackling large, troublesome problems, or a desire to create a flow of empathy between members of both firms).

The cycle of co-creation starts with the *strategic account manager and the senior buyer*. No one is in a better position to initiate co-creation than the two people specifically charged with managing the relationship between supplier and customer. Beyond being initiators of the co-creation, though, the SAM's and senior buyer's roles are to encourage the weaving of numerous *interactions* across (and often within) the two organizations, i.e., they act as networkers tirelessly wiring together previously disconnected members of both organizations. The interactions they foster are based on tackling new subsets of the problem(s) they have chosen to attack. Members of both firms continuously formulate new questions, sometimes in a neutral, open-minded discovery mode, sometimes with a hypothesis or point of view they want to test about a possible solution. Either way, figuring out the answer to the question requires the *use of data*, which may or may not exist through the existing technology platforms already in place at both companies. One of the key roles of SAMs and procurement people is to encourage the development of new data platforms where none historically existed.

Neither SAM nor procurement people engage in co-creation for idealistic reasons; they do so out of sheer self-interest in order to enrich their professional *experience* at their respective firms and to advance their career, starting with trying to reach, or beat, quota for the SAM, or save money for the senior buyer. By so doing, they induce an improvement in the professional experience of other players in both firms, generally allowing the development of win-win relationships where there used to be transactional tug-pulling. Ultimately, the goal of co-creation is to generate a new source of *value* that was previously untapped, and let the SAM and senior buyer figure out how to share it between the two firms through a negotiating process.

The translation of this conceptual definition of co-creation into a phase-by-phase cycle and a description of what skills the SAM and senior buyer need to develop at each phase is outlined below. Here are the ten specific questions you will repeatedly need to answer on the road to co-creation, with the skills you will need to acquire at each step in parentheses.

1. Can we formulate a problem or opportunity that the account manager and procurement agent can solve together? (Become a problem-solver.)
2. How can we identify and recruit a mini-community of people on the supplier and customer required to tackle that problem/opportunity? (Become a community organizer).
3. Can we find a place or "engagement platform" where this mini-community of people can come together in live fashion? (Become an event planner).

4. At the event, how can we help formulate questions or hypotheses the group would like to answer or test with the help of data? (Become a group facilitator).

5. Can we use, or encourage, the development of a technology platform linking the two companies to provide the necessary data? (Become a technology advocate).

6. Can we use the data generated to provide original answers (insights) on the questions or hypotheses you have selected? (Become an analytics story-teller).

7. Can we organize new interactions with new players around the data-driven insights we have generated, thereby redefining the role of sales and procurement? (Become an organizational coach).

8. Can we foster a sense of shared experience across members of both firms as a result of the effort? (Become an empathy bridge-builder).

9. How can we devise a way to share the new value created between supplier and customer? (Become a value innovator).

10. How can we move on to the next-order problem, having earned the right to do so? (Become a transformation agent).

Figure 2.1 illustrates how these ten questions constitute the co-creation cycle

The best way to illustrate the co-creation cycle is to take a real-life example of a company that practices co-creation and reverse-engineer how the SAMs of the company and the procurement managers at the customer firm interact. In this chapter, we will use the case of Ecolab, a $14 B company headquartered in St. Paul, Minnesota,[1] to show what a co-creation model looks like once it reaches maturity. In the rest of this book, we will describe how the co-creation model gradually develops stage by stage, from inception to maturity.

---

[1] For a general introduction to Ecolab, see the company's web site at http://www.ecolab.com/. This chapter was written with the benefit of the operational experience of one of the authors (Francis Gouillart) in operating a large commercial kitchen called Stock Pot Malden in Malden, Massachusetts (www.stockpotmalden.com). Stock Pot Malden is a customer of Ecolab. Francis Gouillart has also been a procurement consultant to a large hotel chain that has a global relationship with Ecolab. In this chapter, we also used the insights of many interviews he conducted during the assignment with this large hotel chain.

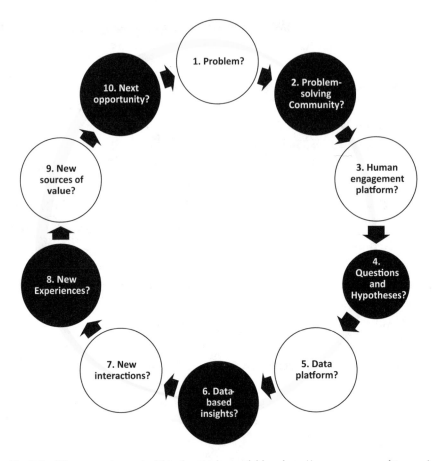

Fig. 2.1 The co-creation cycle. This chart is also available at http://www.eccpartnership.com/the-co-creation-edge.html

Ecolab is best known for its global leadership in cleaning and sanitation services and products for hospitality, foodservice, healthcare and other institutional users. This has been the core business of the firm since it was founded in 1986. Before 2011, the firm grew by expanding organically into new application areas close to its core business. In 2011, though, Ecolab made two major acquisitions that resulted in a dramatic diversification of its portfolio.[2] First, it bought Nalco, a company which, today, anchors Ecolab's new division in the water treatment business catering to large industrial users.[3] In

---

[2] For an account of the role of acquisitions in the success of Ecolab, see for example the Economist's article entitled Cleaning Up, October 2013, available at http://www.economist.com/news/business/21587277-bed-bugs-and-fracking-are-not-only-things-ecolab-has-going-it-cleaning-up.

[3] For a description of Nalco's acquisition by Ecolab, see the Wall Street Journal article entitled Ecolab to acquire Nalco for $5.38B, available at http://www.wsj.com/articles/

2012, it acquired Champion, a firm that has become the heart of Ecolab's new energy business (it largely consists of processing chemicals for the oil and gas industry).[4]

The firm is highly successful by any yardstick of performance: its revenue growth rate has exceeded 20% over the last five years (2010–2014, including the acquisition of Nalco and Champion). Its earnings per share have grown at an annual rate of 18% over the same period, its return on equity has averaged 20%, and its stock price that has been multiplied by 2.6 over those same years.[5]

Ecolab relies on a two-tiered company-owned sales force. The company has corporate account managers who handle the relationship with large institutional chains (these are the people we will focus on in this chapter and refer to as SAMs; it also has a large field sales force that calls on individual units of those large accounts (plants, locations, restaurants, etc.), as well as on fragmented smaller players. In our illustration of how Ecolab follows a cocreative model, we will mostly focus on its historical cleaning and sanitation business, and on the role of the SAMs calling on large food providers, such as restaurant and hotel chains.

So how do the Ecolab SAMs and the senior buyers in corporate restaurant and hotel chains address the 10 questions of our co-creation process?

1   Can We Formulate a Problem or Opportunity that Account Managers and Procurement Agents Can Solve Together? (Become a Problem-Solver)

At the simplest level, Ecolab addresses the problem of keeping commercial kitchens clean and sanitized by providing products, such as dishwashing machines, chemicals, hand soaps, air fresheners, floor cleaners and disinfectants. The Ecolab SAM is in the business of selling products and services that keep commercial kitchens spic-and-span and ensures that the food is safe. Procurement people at the restaurant or hotel chain are in the business of minimizing the cost of an unglamorous (and fairly small) expense category that is typically hidden deep inside the portfolio of a buyer charged with

[4] For a description of Ecolab's acquisition of Champion, see Bloomberg article entitled Ecolab agrees to buy Champion for $2.2B, available at: http://www.bloomberg.com/news/articles/2012-10-12/ecolab-agrees-to-buy-champion-for-2-2-billion-in-cash-and-stock.

[5] Source: authors' analysis of Ecolab annual report and 10K documents.

"ancillary supplies and services" or "indirect spend" (the term "indirect" refers to the fact that the cleaning products or services are not part of the food being sold).

So what keeps the CEO of the restaurant or hotel chain awake at night? It is not spending too much on cleaning supplies. It is the fact that one single kitchen could, one day, serve contaminated food that poisons a large number of customers and creates a huge liability for the company (not to mention exposing the CEO to personal civil or criminal liability). By transforming the agenda from a minor cost problem to a dramatic risk management issue, the Ecolab SAM puts herself in a position to approach her counterpart in corporate procurement and engage him in a discussion of how the two of them can co-create to mitigate this risk.

The Ecolab SAM cannot solve the problem by herself. She knows that Ecolab detergent chemicals and other sanitation products are effective, but reducing the risk of food contamination across all kitchens of the company requires a lot more than selling Ecolab products and services. It necessitates developing a complex set of relationships where all individual kitchen managers learn about food safety, begin tracking data about their safety practices, and are willing to change their mode of operations. Since the SAM and the senior buyer cannot be in all kitchens at all times, they have to rely on others to do the necessary work, with the help of procedures, tools and data that the Ecolab SAM and the restaurant senior buyer devise and utilize jointly to support their work.

Notice how the Ecolab SAM and senior buyer in the restaurant or hotel chain act as *problem-solvers*. At this stage, they're not yet trying to solve the problem as much as formulate it. Great SAMs and great buyers have this in common that they continuously reframe the problem they are trying to solve. The problem is ideally first defined as a narrow issue: "let's work together on how to keep the restaurants' kitchens clean" that will give both parties operational legitimacy, but it can be extended to a broader, and more ambitious, problem statement: "together, we can figure out how to minimize the restaurant chain's risk of major liability of food contamination". The smaller problem statement earns the right to tackle the larger issue, but runs the risk of not being inspirational enough to warrant the mobilization of the other party. The more ambitious formulation of the problem captures the imagination of both the supplier and customer organization and yields fertile ground for a new sales and procurement approach, but its downside is that the supplier may not be able to do anything about the problem, or the ambitious formulation may spook the SAM, or senior buyer counterpart who may not feel he has the legitimacy to tackle something of that magnitude.

Once the minimalist and maximalist problem statements have been articulated, SAMs and senior buyers typically find it easier to fill in the holes between the two extreme problem formulations. For example, Ecolab SAMs now also partner with senior procurement people on issues, such as appliance repairs (fixing broken dishwashers), kitchen productivity (how to minimize staff cost by advising on kitchen layout) or improving sustainability (how to recycle or minimize energy consumption).

2   How Can We Identify and Recruit a Mini-community of People on the Supplier and Customer Required to Tackle that Problem/ Opportunity? (Become a Community Organizer)

On their own, SAMs and senior buyers are powerful, yet lonely professionals. Yes, they are responsible for a large amount of sales and spend at their respective firms. But they cannot do much by themselves. At Ecolab, the role of SAMs and their senior buyer customers is to weave together a network of individuals who, at the local level of each restaurant, helps to figure out how to implement the firm's vision of preventing food contamination wherever it occurs. Let us follow the human dots the SAM and senior buyer must connect to bring the relevant people to the problem-solving party.

Long before engaging the customer, mobilizing the Ecolab internal team around the vision of the problem is the first challenge. Preventing food contamination around the world requires that the Ecolab SAM involve local sales people calling on each restaurant and communicate the problem statement. For a large restaurant chain, this can require engaging (several thousand people). To do so, Ecolab SAMs communicate with their local sales people through a variety of tools (monthly phone calls, common repositories of information, CRM systems with dedicated account areas, etc.). Once they understand the issues they have to solve, local sales people at Ecolab are in a position to call on each kitchen, or supply manager customer, and engage them in a discussion of how to address cleaning and food contamination issues in their kitchen (they already interact frequently as part of the normal sell-buy relationship).

On the customer side, however, the restaurant chain is also concerned with food contamination and will typically have a high-level quality control person, or group, responsible for setting kitchen cleanliness standards and preventing food contamination incidents. Chances are, the quality process of the restaurant chain has a control and compliance bias rather than a problem-solving orientation, and its dynamics are primarily top-down. The process is typically owned by a functional direction at headquarters and cascaded, as policy and procedures, to all kitchen managers in the group. The Ecolab procurement manager interfacing with our SAM will typically not be part of the team that sets those standards, highlighting the first disconnect for the Ecolab SAM: how to convey to the restaurant chain quality team that Ecolab has something to contribute to the setting of their cleanliness and food contamination prevention standards?

One of the ways in which the Ecolab SAM increases her involvement is by introducing the work of the firm's R&D team. Ecolab has about 700 people in R&D worldwide.[6] One of R&D's roles is to develop new products (e.g., detergents) and equipment (e.g., dispensers, dishwasher components) to continuously improve the state of the art in cleaning and food contamination. Ecolab's most successful SAMs have built a connection between Ecolab's R&D group and the senior quality people of their customers, and are able to influence the policies and practices of their corporate clients, utilizing the credibility lent by Ecolab's research and development capability.

The second disconnect in the human chain lies entirely on the customer side: kitchen and supply managers are typically disconnected from each other and do not learn across kitchens in any systematic fashion. Many would like to compare notes with their colleagues at other restaurants (being a restaurant manager is a pretty solitary endeavor), but there is often little time and infrastructure for peer-to-peer dialog. By default, they become passive recipients of directives coming from headquarters, and that is the extent of co-creation at their level. As we shall see a bit later, one of the tools at the disposal of the Ecolab SAMs is a platform that allows them to remotely collect data in each kitchen, share that data with the central procurement and quality control people at the customer's headquarters, and suggest changes back to the individual kitchen managers.

Notice how the Ecolab SAM acts as a *community organizer*. A lot of her time is spent aligning members of her team and the customer team around the problem she wants to tackle. By relentlessly connecting people, she also helps the senior procurement person find a new legitimacy that the buyer

---

[6] Source: Chemical and Engineering News, article entitled Ecolab to buy chemical firm Nalco, July 2011, available at https://pubs.acs.org/cen/news/89/i30/8930notw3.html.

may not have on his own, for example, by reconnecting the procurement person with the technical quality folks at the restaurant chain. Rather than bypassing the buyer, the SAM encourages the senior procurement person to see the value in the Ecolab approach, and inviting him to factor that into the next negotiation, resulting in less focus on price and more on created value.

Exceptional SAMs and senior buyers are uniquely good at including an increasing number of participants in their community. While the traditional sales and procurement approach relies on minimizing the number of decision makers and going *mano-a-mano* with them, the best sales and procurement people recognize that extending the buying and selling network is itself a source of competitive advantage. Contrary to the old selling adage, broadening the sales and procurement network does not result in more people being given a chance to object to the sale (this is only true if the people involved do not add any value). In general, the wider the network of relevant players involved on both sides, the more the SAM and the senior buyer create an unstoppable problem-solving dynamic across supplier and customer.

3   Can We Find a Place or "Engagement Platform" Where This Mini-Community of People Can Come Together in Live Fashion? (Become an Event Planner)

Humans need physical interaction of some kind (this is why solitary confinement is so painful to prisoners submitted to it). At some point, SAMs and senior buyers have to meet physically. No relationship between a SAM and a senior buyer is ever purely virtual. This physical interaction may occur during the quarterly business review between the two firms, or at some supplier conference organized by the buyer, or some large customer gathering organized by the supplier. These live meetings are key moments in the relationship and offer a generally underutilized opportunity to engage in co-creation.

Astute and careful SAMs know how to avoid making such meetings into "death by PowerPoint" presentations of the firm's capabilities. Similarly, senior buyers know to stay away from presentations of requirements and future needs, with an occasional "best supplier award" included as a motivation for senior suppliers to show up. Great SAMs and senior buyers create open agendas, unstructured problem-solving sessions at various levels, and they spend a lot of time orchestrating the physical surrounding of the meeting to encourage give-and-take rather than lectures. They use flip charts and markers by the pool, and spend a lot of time carefully designing breakout groups and report-out procedures in engaging settings, paying great attention to how the physical surroundings will encourage, or deter, the human dialogue. These are skills most commonly found with *event planners*, or even architects, designers or stage directors.

But the live theater of co-creation is not limited to senior meetings between SAMs and senior buyers. At Ecolab, every kitchen of the restaurant or hotel chain is a live engagement platform where local people discuss problems and solutions. Each kitchen has its unique set of equipment, food and staff and the local Ecolab rep must figure out how to best interact with that kitchen's team in its own space and time. Partnering with the local kitchen manager and/or buyer of cleaning products, she must learn when the kitchen is less busy to allow for a surfacing of the latest problems, how to orchestrate the lineup of the relevant parties in the kitchen, and how to choreograph the discussion to create value for the group. The best Ecolab people can frequently be found conducting mini-lectures in a corner of the kitchen, with a small staff huddled around them and engaged in Q&A. This open, generative approach is a far cry from the traditional sales call where the sales person shows up with some detergent products that the buyer purchases when he runs out.

The role of the SAM is to teach every sales person how to orchestrate these live events between sales people and buyers, from the highest level on down to each individual kitchen. She becomes a global event organizer that encourages each sales rep to master the art of physically laying out, in space and time, how the problem-solving will take place to produce the maximum amount of sales. The senior buyer, if he is of the more advanced variety, plays a symmetric role and devises formats and concepts for individual kitchen problem-solving meetings, in partnership with the Ecolab SAM.

4   At the Event, How Can We Help Formulate Questions or Hypotheses the Group Would Like to Answer, or Test, with the Help of Data? (Become a Group Facilitator)

One of the crucial roles of SAMs and senior buyers lies in the art of formulating questions. Not any questions, mind you, questions which can be answered through the use of data. Here are some examples of questions the Ecolab SAMs ask (and ask their teams to ask at the local level):

- How can we reduce the dishwashing cost of all your kitchens?
- How can we reduce manpower costs in your kitchens?

- How can we reduce the energy costs everywhere?
- How can we minimize downtime of your dishwashing machines?
- How can we prevent food contamination at the corporate level?

Notice that these are questions that the senior buyer at the hotel, or restaurant chain, should be asking long before the Ecolab SAMs asks them, because senior buyers are the ones who own those issues. In practice, senior buyers often do not have the analytical disposition or the operational experience to get to that level of granularity. Most senior buyers aim for broad "spend reduction", but they rarely know enough to break down the problem into its analytical components, let alone figure out what data would be required to address the issue. This is where the Ecolab SAM (or local sales rep) whispers in their ears what questions they should ask their suppliers, whether in a formal RFP, or in general consultations. Of course, the Ecolab SAM and local sales people know that by supplying the questions, they dramatically increase the chances of Ecolab making the sale, since the firm is uniquely good at answering those questions through the capabilities it brings.

Learning how to frame questions so they can be answered with real data that only your firm can provide (and ultimately showing that Ecolab will save money for the restaurant or hotel chain in documented fashion) does not necessarily come easy to sales people historically trained in the art of "processing to yes", or creating leading narratives designed to overcome objections. Instead of using scripted narratives and railroading processes, they need to become *group facilitators* comfortable with open-ended agendas where members of the supplier and customer teams roam freely toward an eventual solution. The role of SAMs and senior buyers is to frame the discussion through the question-led process, feature experts from their firm, where appropriate, and act as effective brokers between the questions posed by the customer and the solutions brought by the supplier.

5 Can We Use, or Encourage, the Development of a Technology Platform Linking the Two Companies to Secure the Necessary Data? (Become a Technology Advocate)

In Chap. 1, we saw that data plays an increasing role in the selling and buying relationship, a phenomenon often described as Big Data. SAMs and senior buyers play a key role in taking the Big Data trend from hype to reality. Ecolab shows how Big Data can be taken from a broad promise to the down-

and-dirty reality (literally) of a restaurant or hotel kitchen. Here is how they do it.

Ecolab has developed a data platform called APEX®. Here is how Ecolab describes APEX® in its promotional literature[7]:

Apex® is a revolutionary new ware-washing platform. Apex® combines state-of-the-art technology with innovative tools and superior products, all backed by personalized service and expertise, to minimize both the total cost of ware-washing and its environmental impact.

Simply put, the Apex® system provides the platform and data that answer the operational questions we asked earlier in our process about equipment, staff efficiency and food contamination risk. It allows the kitchen staff, with the help of the local Ecolab sales person, to continuously discover new avenues for kitchen productivity improvements and risk minimization. For example, the Apex® platform analyzes the use and efficiency of each piece of cleaning and sanitizing equipment in the kitchen, answering questions such as "how frequently was this dishwasher used?", "how many racks or dishes were washed on average in this machine?", or "what was the temperature curve for each dishwashing cycle?"

While this may look like gratuitously detailed data to the uninitiated, the percent utilization for each piece of equipment drives the efficiency of capital allocation for the hotel or restaurant chain, answering the question: "When should we authorize this particular kitchen to spend money on a new piece of equipment?" The analysis of the temperature curve is what answers the question: "How do we make sure that we have killed all the food bacteria and are, therefore, mitigating the risk of food contamination?" The Apex® platform also tracks data pertaining to water consumption, energy use and staff time associated with cleaning and sanitizing. The platform can display this data over multiple months and shows trends, providing fodder for discussions between kitchen staff and Ecolab sales reps on how to improve operations and minimize risk.

What is the role of the Ecolab SAM and the senior buyer in connection with Apex®? Their role is to encourage use of the platform at the individual kitchen level, which requires providing "data religion" to local sales reps (for

[7] For a description of Apex, see Ecolab's brochure entitled Apex 2: More Control, Made Simple, available at: http://video.ecolab.com/wp-content/uploads/Apex2Overview Brochure042012-2.pdf.

the SAM) and kitchen managers (for senior buyers). It also involves training them in the use and interpretation of the data, a mammoth educational task from an implementation standpoint, since neither Ecolab sales people, nor average kitchen managers, are typically recruited because of their analytical depth. This new world challenges them to become *technology advocates*. Their role is to lead their respective teams to the data well, and encourage them to devise creative new improvement paths based on that data. They are not expected to be technology experts—the actual development of the platform is left to IT and R&D people at Ecolab—but they are expected to provide field-based feedback on the user-friendliness of the technology and on new features their daily customers would like to see added.

6 Can We Use the Data Generated to Create Insights into How the Questions or Hypotheses Can Be Answered or Validated? (Become an Analytics Story-Teller)

Once the technology is in place and data has begun to accumulate, the SAM and the senior buyer need to start making sense out of that data. Most importantly, they need to teach every sales rep and local buyer how to do the same in the unique context of each kitchen in the restaurant or hotel chain. This is one of the most difficult steps in the co-creation process: generating insights from the data.

Although there are highly sophisticated ways to look at data by developing fancy statistical models, the simplest way to think of insights is to think in terms of correlation, i.e., try to figure out "what drives what?". For the more mathematically inclined, this is taught in high school and college math as building a regression model, i.e., try to predict a variable (say, the total cost of running a kitchen), by relating it to some other variable such as "having a unique, skilled operator to run the dishwasher", "ensuring that the dishwasher is full every time you run it", or "setting the dishwasher temperature at a certain level"). Once they get the hang of it, sales reps and kitchen managers can start identifying all kinds of variables they feel may help their operation from a cost or efficiency standpoint, then assess whether it produces the desirable outcome of reducing the cost (or minimize breakdowns of equipment, or prevent food incidents).

Bear in mind that the hard part is never the mathematical testing of the idea (there are lots of data experts who can do that). The hard part is to develop an intuition for what might be related to what. And who is best qualified to have this intuition? It is the operating people in the kitchen, of course, since they live in that world every day. What they don't have is a language to frame their ideas, and a platform to collect the data that will test their ideas. Until Apex®, that is. The role of the Ecolab sales person is to teach them that with Apex®, they can now create these hypotheses and test them.

Notice that the data-based dialogue occurs at two levels: a local level and a global level. At the local level, each kitchen team and Ecolab sales person is encouraged to develop their own insights for their particular kitchen. Since each kitchen is different in terms of layout, age of equipment, or skills of staff, they will come up with their own recipe for improvement. One might call this Small Data, since there is no expectation that what is found to be true for that particular kitchen in Iowa is applicable to all other kitchens of the restaurant or hotel chain.

At the global level, the Ecolab SAM and his senior buyer counterpart can aggregate the data across all kitchens and start seeing general patterns that result in universal rules that can be cascaded back to all kitchens. For example, the Ecolab SAMs have learned that the total cost of cleaning and sanitizing a kitchen is driven by the cost of the Ecolab supplies (what they sell to the restaurant or hotel kitchen), the amount of staff used to manage cleaning and supplies, water consumption costs, energy costs and equipment maintenance and replacement costs. With the support of some analytics people, they have created normative models, or benchmarks, of what each of these costs should be, given certain characteristics of the kitchen, and can offer "top-down" prescriptions on what to do if some numbers deviate strongly from the mean. For example, they will suggest an energy training program for the staff if they discover the energy cost to be out of line, or some upgrade of the warewashing equipment.

Repeatedly, we have found that improvements resulting from Small Data are greater than ones resulting from Big Data. In other words, the size of improvement generated at the level of an individual kitchen by the Ecolab sales rep and the kitchen staff (with the help of a platform like Apex®) is larger and more sustainable than the one resulting from the grand mathematical model in the sky developed by aggregating the data from all kitchens. Why? The answer is both objective and behavioral. All kitchens are different and bringing a common universal prescription across a rainbow of kitchen types can only take you so far. Second, it is a lot more rewarding for local Ecolab sales reps and kitchen staffs to implement something they generated, rather than mindlessly cascading a practice developed by an anonymous team at headquarters.

Great SAMs and senior buyers have a unique ability when it comes to data and insights: they transform the nerdy numbers into great anecdotes that give you the desire to go try it yourself. They are *analytics story-tellers*. They do not rely on mathematical models as much as on the story of how some 22-year-old kid in Nashville transformed the whole operations of the kitchen by showing tattooed prep people and chefs how to run the machine differently. They convert boring left-brained insights on cost reduction and food safety risk minimization into human interest stories that potential customers are motivated to repeat and eventually become part of.

7   Can We Organize New Interactions with New Players Around the Data-Driven Insights You Have Generated? (Become an Organizational Coach)

SAMs and senior buyers need to continuously produce new insights at the intersection of their firms. There may be excitement if new insights get generated once, but absent a steady flow of new ideas, the initial enthusiasm will fizzle out back and the old transactional relationship will return.

To sustain the co-creation process, Ecolab SAMs rely on their local sales teams to encourage the formation of problem-solving teams inside each kitchen (in practice, this happens mostly in larger kitchens), with each team specializing on generating specific streams of improvements inside the larger productivity model. These teams are permanent structures, although their focus changes as a function of the problems at hand. For teams to be effective, they need a charter (what are they are tasking themselves to do), a governance structure with some senior access to provide resources or remove implementation obstacles, some project management structure (who is in charge on the supplier and customer side?), a defined mode of working (frequency of meetings, place, agenda), supporting infrastructure (what data are brought to what meeting?), and some accounting for results (how will they track the benefits they generate?). Someone needs to do this structuring work, and it falls naturally to SAMs and senior buyers to design those interactions, and encourage their respective teams to replicate this structure wherever possible at the local level.

One hotel chain, for example, has an equipment team focused on capital expenditures and capacity utilization, a team focused on energy, another group focused on water, one on staff productivity and one on food safety.[8] The structure of those teams has been heavily influenced by the Ecolab SAM who convinced his senior buyer counterpart at the hotel chain that this is the best way to allocate responsibilities to generate the intended cost reductions. The local sales reps make sure the teams utilize the relevant Apex® data, whenever available, for their specific kitchen, occasionally contribute benchmark data from the corporate Ecolab performance database, and frequently participate in their customers' weekly, or bi-weekly, problem-solving sessions aimed at improving performance. Needless to say, the local Ecolab rep enjoys a tremendous competitive advantage vs. her competition by having access to the thinking of the kitchen team and being in a position to influence their next move.

For this to happen, SAMs and sales reps need to be *organizational designers*, and the same is true for senior buyers who work with them on the customer side. Neither party has any hierarchical legitimacy to suggest to kitchen operations people why they should undertake this improvement process, how they should structure their teams, who should sit on them, how they should track results, and why they should find the time to do this data-driven work when they're already swamped by cooking work in the first place. And yet, this is exactly what great SAMs and senior buyers manage to do; they get kitchen teams to pay attention to a lot of details that ultimately results in a significant performance improvement in cleaning and sanitizing those kitchens.

8   Can We Foster a Sense of Shared Experience Across Members of Both Firms as a Result of the Effort? (Become an Empathy Bridge-Builder)

So why do SAMs and senior buyers go through this trouble of jointly defining problems, building communities on both sides of the aisle, framing questions, bringing data and orchestrating a soul-searching process to generate original answers to new problems? They do so because it is a lot more fun for them to work in this fashion and help each other succeed than to beat each other up in a transactional lose-lose battle. Most people prefer having friends than enemies. The majority of us pick shared prosperity over fights about spoils of war, if given a chance.

---

[8] Source: confidential interviews done by one of the authors (Francis Gouillart) during a procurement project done for a large global hotel chain.

SAMs and senior procurement managers seek to create a happy professional experience, both for themselves and for the other party. A happy professional experience comes from two sources: an objective, quantitatively measurable sense of corporate achievement; and a more personal, qualitative, feeling-driven sense of self-worth and meaning. On the objective quantitative front, Ecolab SAMs derive pleasure from achieving, or beating, their sales targets, which fuels their ability to make good money through salary, bonus and advancement. Their ability to achieve those quantitative results is the result of producing value for their respective companies as a whole, and represents their "share of the corporate loot" (of course, there are huge variations across corporations in the ways SAM and senior buyer compensation plans are structured to link individual compensation to corporate value produced). This financial reward is the result of the co-creative work they do. On the procurement side, buyers are similarly rewarded economically by achieving, or beating, their spend reduction targets.

The qualitative rewards are subtler. The personal experience of the SAM and the senior buyer are inextricably linked: they win or lose together. There is a notable empathy that links great SAMs and high-performing senior buyers. They "feel" for each other, and are confident enough in each other to be transparent about their respective status, or ambition, inside their company. They have a sense of shared destiny. Many Ecolab SAMs build their annual account plan with large customers in cooperative fashion and jointly create sales and procurement spending targets. Some go as far as to make transparent the implications of these numbers to their compensation or career ambition, bringing a new level of intimacy to the relationship. Most importantly, the SAM never tries to marginalize, or eliminate, the senior buyer from the process, by end-running him and going directly to corporate quality or risk people on food safety issues, for example. Ecolab SAMs also build relationships with many other parties besides the procurement people, but they are careful to do this in cooperation with senior buyers, rather than by bypassing them.

The business-to-business world has been slow to acknowledge this more emotional side of the SAM-senior buyer relationship, as if the combination of business and feelings was structurally inadvisable, or worse yet, unethical. Nothing could be more wrong. There is plenty of room for emotional issues in business, and the best SAMs and senior buyers are inevitably *empathetic leaders* who are not afraid to become personal in their discussions. They exhibit confidence in certain areas, vulnerability in others, and constantly try to help the professional life of the other party. Furthermore, they encourage their sales and procurement teams at the local level to develop similarly empathic, win-win relationships and to become more personal. They are also good at motivating the other party to embrace a broad formulation of the problems they are trying to solve. The best Ecolab SAMs talk about food safety as a societal challenge the world needs to embrace, which, for senior buyers, is a lot more motivational than reducing spending on detergents and sanitizers (although the latter is also important).

This empathetic quality is frequently found with people with a traditional sales background, leading some pundits to characterize this skill as an attribute of old-fashioned salesmanship that is no longer pertinent in the more data-driven modern world of the SAM and the senior buyer. In reality, both the empathetic and data skills are needed, requiring great SAMs and senior buyers to be not only right- or left-brained, but whole-brained.

9   How Can We Devise a Way to Share the New Value Created Between Supplier and Customer? (Become a Value Innovator)

At the end of the day, no matter how co-creative their relationship is, SAMs and senior buyers still have to conduct a tough negotiation. The only difference from the traditional approach is that there is now new value to be divided. This new value allows, but does not guarantee, the eventual outcome is win-win (there may still be a disproportionate amount of value accruing to one side or the other as a result of the negotiation). Before the negotiation itself, though, the important part is to figure out how to document the value created, a far from trivial task. In a successful relationship between the Ecolab SAM and the senior buyer at a large restaurant or hotel chain, new value is constantly being created in six areas, all of which must be documented in spite of the fact that the owners of each benefit area can be located in different places inside the customer company:

1. The joint team improves utilization of the existing kitchen equipment, which results in either delaying the need to buy new machines (reduced capital expenditures of interest to the CFO), or allowing a larger volume of dishes to be cleaned and sanitized in that kitchen without increase in cost (operating cost avoidance in the P&L of the kitchen manager).

2. The amount of detergent products used per unit of output (say, per rack or dish) is constantly lowered. Notice that the total Ecolab sales

may still be going up if total production of the kitchen increases and/or the market share of Ecolab within that kitchen increases, allowing the Ecolab SAM to still register growth in the account, while the senior buyer shows a reduction in total per unit spending. The lower use of detergents is typically recognized as a cost reduction in the kitchen's profit and loss statement cost and as an environmental item owned by the Chief Sustainability Officer (CSO) of the hotel or restaurant chain.

3. The labor cost associated with cleaning or sanitizing is reduced because fewer people are needed. This item is owned by the person who manages the kitchen's P&L and its labor line item.

4. The total amount of water consumed is steadily being reduced. There again, hotel and restaurant chains care about water both from a cost (kitchen P&L) and from an environmental footprint standpoint (CSO agenda).

5. The energy consumption keeps going down. Once again, the benefit is typically counted both as an operational cost reduction for the kitchen, and as an environmental item owned by the CSO.

6. The food contamination risk is reduced by the better procedures. The interested parties for this item are typically the senior executive in charge of kitchen operations and quality assurance, or the risk management function inside the CFO area.

So how do the Ecolab SAM and the senior buyer in a hotel or restaurant chain keep track of the value created in those various areas (kitchen P&L. environmental scorecard, risk mitigation for CFO)? And how does this value get shared effectively between the two firms? In an ideal world, the Ecolab SAM and the senior buyer would be in a position to quantify the value created in all six areas in all kitchens of the hotel or restaurant chain. They would be able to aggregate that value, and Ecolab and its customer would then agree to divide it through a negotiation process, ending up with some division of the value created, say 50%–50%. Each sale of detergent or service would then be considered an investment in reducing cost or risk, and quantified as such. While this is where Ecolab would ideally like to go, today's reporting reality does not yet allow this massive aggregation of value and the negotiated sharing of that value between Ecolab and its customers.

What takes place, instead, is a more traditional negotiation on price and quantities. The main difference with the old-fashioned commodity transaction, though, is that both the Ecolab SAM and the senior buyer at the restaurant or hotel chain are cognizant of the value that has been created by the Ecolab approach. This effectively reduces the credibility of any competitive threat and gives strong leverage to Ecolab in the negotiation, in terms of higher prices and larger quantities. As a result, Ecolab is perceived as quite expensive compared to competitors, which is made possible by the fact that it creates a lot more value than its competitor. Its market share has also been steadily increasing at most large accounts, as a reward for the value it creates for its customers.

The role of the SAM and the senior buyer is that of a *value innovator*. On one end, they negotiate price and quantities with each other in the traditional way (they must read each other's position and assess what each other's next best alternative is, and propose or accept offers accordingly). The main skill SAMs and buyers exhibit in the new environment, though, lies in their ability to document the value they have created through this new, innovative approach. Raw negotiation skills still matter, but showing up with documented evidence that value has been created is where the true negotiating leverage lies. One of the greatest attributes of value documentation is that it puts SAMs and senior buyers on the same side of the table (the senior buyer's task is also made easier by the fact that he can show the rest of his customer organization what value has been created). After that, there is still a hard-nosed negotiation to be conducted, but doing so based on the common acceptance that value has been created makes it much easier.

10 How Can We Move on to the Next-Order Problem, Having Earned the Right to Do So? (Become a Transformation Agent)

Over time, the SAM and the senior buyer earn each other's trust, allowing them to tackle more and more ambitious problems and to create increasing value. At that moment, their agenda often moves from a purely operational improvement, cost-dominated one to a strategic model where revenue generation and joint developments also play an important part. In some cases, their work extends all the way to the creation of a new business model for both firms, or at least involves some experimentation leading to such a model. SAMs and senior buyers sometimes conceptualize this progression as a value stairway, with each plank of value building on the preceding one. Others prefer visualizing concentrating circles of value of increasing radius (this is the representation we will use in this book, and Chap. 10 offers such a visualization of increasing value in five circles). Whatever representation is selected, they start articulating a long-term transformation plan for their respective firms.

At Ecolab, the value circle starts with reducing the cost of cleansing and sanitizing materials consumed, which requires optimizing the storage and use of the chemicals themselves. The next value circle involves improving utilization of the existing equipment, teaching staff to reduce labor and energy costs associated with the running of the machines. The third circle involves preventing the breakdown of equipment through proper maintenance and installing new equipment where needed, while changing kitchen processes and layout where necessary. The ultimate circle of value involves having the Ecolab SAM and the senior buyer at the hotel, or restaurant chain partner, develop, and put in place, an integrated food safety process across all locations to reduce the food contamination risk and any potential liabilities associated with it.

Once they have developed the required intimacy, the role of the SAM and senior buyer becomes one of *transformation agent*. They are no longer mere sellers and buyers of products and services, but they become architects of the change agenda of their respective firms. Together, they articulate what value can be created at the intersection of their respective firms, sell their management on the agenda they have created, and mobilize the necessary resources on both sides to make it happen. In their transformational role, they continuously launch new experiments whose outcome is to gradually change their firm's business model. The best SAMs know that "you are what you sell", i.e., a firm's business model evolves with each innovatively constructed sale the firm makes.

In Chap. 3, we turn to the chronology of implementation of the co-creation model, discovering how the SAM and senior buyer go through the cycle of co-creation differently depending on where they are in the strategic relationship-building process.

CHAPTER 3

The Strategic Relationship-Building Process

In the previous chapter we described the cycle of co-creation that takes place between advanced SAMs and high-performing senior buyers. This cycle gets repeated over time between supplier and customer, producing results of increasing magnitude as they build trust with each other. For example, the strategic relationship between Ecolab SAMs and senior buyers, like Rome, was not built in one day. It developed over many years between Ecolab and its customers. In this third chapter, we describe the six steps through which a strategic relationship between a supplier and a customer grows over time.

A typical relationship-building process involves six steps describing what the SAM and senior buyer do at that stage. Each stage in the relationship between the SAM and the senior buyer (and the rest of their respective organizations) can be compared to the development of a romantic relationship between two people, from the very early stages of dreamy aspirations to the development of an actual relationship and the forming of a family. Here are the six steps:

1. The Dream: Discover the Opportunity and Organize Internally
2. The Dance: Envision the Value and Assemble a Joint Team
3. The Date: Engage as One Team and Connect Emotionally
4. The Commitment: Finalize Value, Negotiate and Close
5. The Long-Term Relationship: Deliver and Document Value
6. The Family: Expand Value

The cycle of co-creation we described in the preceding chapter is repeated at each step, as illustrated in Fig. 3.1.

To illustrate the strategic relationship process involved, we show how a strategic account manager in one of the divisions of Techelec Electric developed a co-creative relationship with a large US oil & gas refiner we call O&G.[1] In this chapter, we tell the story from the perspective of the supplier.

Techelec Electric is a large automation and energy management company.[2] The business we focus on in this chapter is the Process Automation unit, which defines its business as enabling safe, reliable and efficient operations for the processing plants of its customers. Even more specifically, we focus here on oil and gas refineries applications (although Techelec's Process Automation division also serves chemical, pulp and paper, steel, and many other continuous process plants). Techelec's processing division develops and sells process

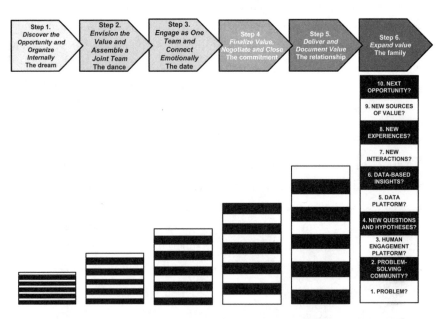

Fig. 3.1 How the co-creation cycle grows at each step of the relationship-building cycle. This chart is also available at http://www.eccpartnership.com/the-co-creation-edge.html

[1] This chapter is adapted from a case previously published by Velocity Magazine, a publication from the Strategic Account Management Association (SAMA), on May 5, 2013.
[2] The name of the actual company has been changed for confidentiality reason. This case is based on several hours of conversation with various managers of the companies involved.

control devices and integrated systems that help its customers' plants run safely and efficiently, as well as software that can be used to design or manage operations for the processing plants. The story described in this chapter is representative of the work done by the strategic accounts team of Techelec, which represented at the time about 15% of total sales of the firm.

1   The Dream: Discover the Opportunity and Get Organized

The first job of a SAM is to discover the business of the potential customer and to identify what issues it faces with the hope of identifying solutions the supplier may be able to provide. This is first done internally, through investigation of public documents about the customer company, without any direct interaction with the customer (the fact that the co-creation process starts through purely internal research may appear paradoxical, but you first need to figure out what you want to co-create with your customers). Beyond defining the problems themselves, it involves trying to identify who "owns" those problems at the customer level. At this stage, little is typically known about the problem or the people who care about them, but the SAM's role is to develop early ideas from research, both Internet-based and ears to the ground on routine sales calls.

The goal is to figure out how to engage customers in a joint discovery process that will ultimately result in the creation of measurable value for the company and some emotional rewards for the people who take the risk to collaborate with the SAM. Of course, the SAM cannot simply pick up the phone and plead for an entirely new way of doing business. The SAM has to construct hypotheses about where the value is likely to be for the customer, as well as for his company (at this stage, the value is conceptual and not yet quantified). The role of research is to help figure out where the value might lie, and to create enough intrigue and interest around it to draw one or two key people in the customer's organization to be willing to embark on an exploration journey.

In Techelec's case, our account manager (we will call him "SAM' for short) was focused on one particular account, O&G Refining, the refinery division of a large American petroleum companies.[3] Techelec had no relationship with that account and had tried to penetrate the company for years without suc-

---

[3] To understand the role of refining in the portfolio of an integrated oil and gas company, see for example https://en.wikipedia.org/wiki/Petroleum_industry.

cess. O&G's technical people were not easily accessible to Techelec, with a "no supplier can teach us how to run our refineries" attitude, a position which was further reinforced by the procurement organization acting as gate-keeper. As a result, O&G had the reputation of being tough in negotiation, transaction-driven and not particularly attractive as a co-creation candidate.

This is where a bit of business intelligence can go a long way. Our SAM heard that O&G had set up "Functional Excellence Teams" tasked with improving various areas of operations at O&G. He figured these new teams might become the right organizational partner for a refinery initiative where Techelec could play a role. He got in touch with one of those teams, the Operations Efficiency Team, and convinced himself there might be a new opportunity there.

Knowing any strategic opportunity with O&G might require significant investment on the Techelec technical side, SAM began seeking executive "air cover". He and his boss, the SAM program head, soon secured the support of the Americas-region president for the O&G initiative. SAM and his boss also enlisted the support of the portfolio management team, ensuring—they hoped—that their project would find its way into the project prioritization pipeline once it was fully baked. They also knew that, before SAM's team could even begin tackling O&G's problem, they would have to build a compelling business case to justify the investment of resources. Our SAM did not yet have a problem identified, nor did he fully understand what the Functional Excellence Teams were about, but he guessed there was someone at the other end of the line willing to engage with him.

2   *The Dance: Envision the Value and Assemble a Joint Team*

And so they danced.

SAM knew that identifying a burning problem to O&G and solving it with Techelec technology would require bringing together multiple stakeholders on both sides of the customer-supplier divide. Good SAMs are tireless choreographers of new interactions between people with unresolved issues on the customer side and people with solution ideas on their company's side. Problems are rarely articulated to the point where packaged solutions magically fit in. And solutions are rarely perfectly packaged to fit neatly into a customer issue. The trick for the SAM is to get both parties to engage with each other and design their dance. Don't expect love at first sight, but over time, both problem and solution may transform their respective shape so as to fit neatly with each other, through the subtle guidance of SAM and senior buyer.

SAM spent a lot of time networking inside O&G's refinery team and learned there were, in fact, multiple Functional Excellence Teams (FETs) comprising a mix of O&G engineering, process, maintenance and operations people whose role was to discover ways to improve operations. Buried deep inside of these FETs, SAM discovered a person acting as "lead for field devices", a particularly relevant job title at Techelec, since the company designs and manufactures many such field devices. SAM now had a target stakeholder to focus on.

He invited the field devices specialist on a customer tour of Techelec's Massachusetts facilities. One of their stop was Techelec's analytical measurement group. "I didn't even know you had an analytical measurement group," SAM remembers O&G's field devices guy saying. SAM knows how to recognize an opening when he sees one, and so he pounced.

"Do you have a specific analytical question you're trying to solve?" he remembers asking in response. The answer: "As a matter of fact, we do." It turns out O&G had been wrestling for years with a problem with one of its hydrofluoric alkylation units.[4]

SAM had seen his share of alkylation units in his career and knew how fickle they can be. Sitting deep inside refineries, they involve chemical reactors that play a key role in the transformation of crude oil into the various grades of gasoline we buy at the pump. (The higher the gasoline grade produced by the reactor, the more profitable the unit.) But there's a catch: An alkylation unit requires using hydrofluoric or sulfuric acid as a catalyst to "high-grade" the gasoline, and these acids are extremely toxic for humans and highly corrosive for equipment. For the unit operator, the name of the game is to inject as much acid as possible while avoiding "acid runaway", the point at which the acid becomes hard to control and can create a quality and safety problem.

To prevent acid runaway, an operator needs to know what's going on inside the reactor. To do so, he has to don full-body protective gear while taking samples of the process and then send samples to a distant lab, where an analytical expert measures various characteristics of the sample with a chro-

---

[4] For a general description of alkylation units, see https://en.wikipedia.org/wiki/Alkylation_unit.

matograph—from which he deduces whether the mix inside the reactor is still safe and stable.

The traditional method of online measurement requires equipment that costs about $1.5 million and needs to be overhauled every two years. It also requires a dedicated maintenance person, in addition to the sample collector. O&G's engineering staff had looked at myriad technical solutions to replace the daily physical collection with a safer, cheaper and more continuous analytical process—all to no avail.

SAM knew in a heartbeat the visit had been worthwhile. He and his team now had a problem they could work to solve for their customer.

SAM and his team argued internally that, if Techelec could devise a compelling technical solution to O&G's alkylation problem, then they could bank on sales of several hundred thousand dollars for each alkylation unit like it in the world—offering the promise of a potential $10 million windfall for Techelec. This was a very crude calculation, but this was value, if he ever saw it.

Aligning the technical constituencies inside Techelec was the next challenge. SAM painstakingly enlisted the support of the analytical measurement group that first caught the customer's eye during that visit in Massachusetts. He lined up the field technician they would need for the work at the refinery with the alkylation unit problem; the manager of the consulting service group that would work with the team on the alkylation problem; the software team in California; and the advanced process controls team that would, in due time, see how the solution being developed could be transformed from an analytical measurement system into a plant optimization process that would safely push the performance of the unit to new levels. And this A-Team represented just the Techelec side of the equation.

On O&G's side, SAM had to start at the top. Involving the senior management of Techelec had earned SAM the right to meet with some of the senior refining executives on the customer side. It was a guarded meeting, SAM recalls. At the time of the meeting, O&G thought of Techelec as an arm's-length supplier, not a partner, with no technical collaboration agreement in place. They did, encouragingly, agree that if Techelec could solve their problem, this would give Techelec credibility as a full-fledged technical partner and not merely a transactional supplier.

Procurement and engineering had been the traditional port of call for Techelec salespeople, and they played their price- and service-level negotiation roles with bruising enthusiasm. But SAM had worked hard at building other connection points in the organization, points of contact he knew would be invaluable in his current pursuit. He had already identified the Refining Business Improvement organization and two of its key FETs: the Process Operations Team and the Field Instrumentation Team. His next step was to see what O&G's Central Engineering Team thought of the project. To his dismay, the team expressed extreme pessimism toward the project based on the history of failed attempts to fix the refining group's alkylation problems. When SAM asked for permission to visit O&G's Texas plant with the alkylation problem, they grudgingly agreed. Given the tepid endorsement from the refining group's central engineering people, the plant operators were commensurately lukewarm. Their attitude, SAM recalls, boiled down to "Come back and see us when you have a solution."

The dance had not yet produced a romantic spark, at best an agreement to meet again and see what would develop.

3   The Date: Engage as One Team and Connect Emotionally

One of the key roles of the SAM is to find a physical place or platform through which the supplier and customer team can start working with each other and learn to like each other. While we often pretend that business-to-business relationships are exclusively about the rational pursuit of economic value, great SAMs and senior buyers know that personal emotions play an important part in the development of strategic relationships. As the old sales adage has it, "people buy things from people they like." SAMs and senior buyers know that they do not have to be the people personally experiencing the flow of empathy (although it helps); their role is to encourage such a connection between people in their respective organizations, not necessarily themselves.

Over a period of months, Techelec's SAM scouted both his own organization and O&G's organization, seeking individuals who could charge the rational problem of the alkylation's unit safety with a personal passion and urgency. SAM's breakthrough came from a connection he orchestrated between two extraordinary individuals, on the customer and Techelec side.

During one of his visits at the targeted Texas refinery, he'd seen firsthand the onerous steps required to fully protect the O&G employee responsible for sampling the troubled alkylation unit. Considering Techelec's stated core mission is to enable safe, reliable and efficient operations for its customers, SAM couldn't help but think that what he'd witnessed was none of the three. There was, he knew, a potentially huge strategic opportunity to make a difference for Techelec at the refiner.

Now this is where our story becomes personal, highlighting as it does the key role a SAM must play in connecting the human passions and expertise of multiple people in the co-creation process. While working on the alkylation problem, SAM had developed great respect for one of O&G's operators, whom he saw regularly during on-site visits. While not a degreed individual, this operator had developed an intense passion for improving the operations of the alkylation units and had transformed himself into a go-to expert on the hydrofluoric alkylation process. SAM made an early mental note of this key personnel discovery, hoping to eventually pair him with an equally motivated and knowledgeable partner on the Techelec solution development side.

Playing detective in his own organization, SAM found his "man on the inside" in the form of a scientist in Techelec's analytical measurement team. Speaking with him, SAM discovered that the scientist had developed a theory whereby two separate measurements relevant to the alkylation problem could be combined to generate a third one, which he believed could hold the key to continuously measuring the state of alkylation process inside a reactor—holding the promise of removing all physical human intervention in the process, with its tremendous safety and cost implications. SAM knew he had the perfect co-creative catalyst in the form of the scientist, who clearly craved a testing ground for his novel hypothesis. The operator at the customer's alkylation unit and the Techelec scientist represented an odd couple in many ways, yet they both played a key role in energizing the broad community of players the SAM orchestrated.

"Without these two people," SAM says, "We would never have gotten there."

In the end, the solution to the refinery's problem turned out to be a Techelec-proprietary process measurement system (a technology "platform") that continuously generates data on what goes on inside the reactor. More precisely, it measures the amount of acid, water and what is known as "acid-soluble oils." It involves an integrated panel-mounted system that is installed in the alkylation unit, which continuously measures the flow and output of the reactor, ensuring that operations are proceeding smoothly. Since it's a direct chemical measurement, no physical human intervention is required– no more full-body suit.

They had now dated. Two highly respected people on each side of the organization were prepared to vouch for the fact they had found a solution to a long-standing problem. They had created a win-win together.

4   The Commitment: Finalize Value, Negotiate and Close

The ultimate purpose of co-creation is to identify and capture value for both sides. For the SAM, this means selling more business and growing the account faster than a normal sales approach would produce. For the senior buyer, this means reducing cost, reducing risk or increasing revenues in some fashion. Once value has been created, it must be measured, then distributed, between supplier and customer. The negotiating skills of the traditional sales and procurement person do not go away. It's just that more value has been created than can be shared, making a win-win possible, but not guaranteeing it (the negotiation) can still produce a winner and a loser in the appropriation of that value.

As a general rule, co-creation business cases tend to have multiple layers of value for both supplier and customer, and this value typically expands over time, as we shall see in the subsequent section.

In the case of Techelec, SAM generated immediate value for the refinery in three areas:

- The new system dramatically reduced the risk for the refiner. The Techelec solution reduced safety exposure by lowering the frequency of testing and analysis of results. The new real-time measurement system produced a dramatic improvement in the alkylation unit's risk grade.
- The new platform cut operational costs by reducing use of the lab chromatograph and the associated manpower and maintenance expenses. It also eliminated the need for the full-time, high-qualification operator who previously handled maintenance on the installation.
- Finally, it allowed the refiner to increase revenues by producing a higher-grade, more valuable gasoline through the use of what is known as "advanced process controls." Thanks to the data produced by the on-line process control system, the reactor can be pushed closer to its limits

without triggering the acid runaway O&G feared when operators had access only to periodic sampling of the liquid inside the reactor.

Meanwhile, Techelec initially created value for itself by making a sale:

- The Techelec SAM sold the first unit of the new system at the Texas refinery where the technology was developed, generating a sale of several hundred thousand dollars with a high margin, as a reflection of the fact that there was no alternative to the Techelec technology solution.

Both parties happily closed the contract and agreed this first commitment might be the beginning of a beautiful story.

5 The Long-Term Relationship: Deliver and Document Value

Closing a contract is one thing. Delivering the promised value is another. Great SAMs know that delivering value today is what produces tomorrow's sales and they pay close attention to putting in place a strong value measurement platform. This is not a trivial problem and it often requires developing, and putting in place, a sensor-based system that captures real-time data, a potentially significant investment. (In the case of Techelec, the firm's entire business is platform-based, so the measurement of value is made possible by the product itself, but for many other companies, this is not the case and the value measurement platform must be developed separately). Measured value then becomes the focus of quarterly business meetings with the customer, allowing greater and greater penetration inside the account and fueling sales growth. Data also has an infectious characteristic: the more data you have, the more new ideas for value you can generate across supplier and customer, and the greater the share of wallet inside the account becomes.

Building a value tracking system requires the careful orchestration of multiple new interactions between members of both firms on both sides. This is a key step as many data-generating platforms set across suppliers and customers remain underutilized, often because nobody was trained on using the data on the customer side, which makes the investment in the platform unproductive and prevents account growth. At Techelec, SAM and his team made sure everybody was trained in understanding the value of the new data being generated.

Now compare the nature of interactions between our various protagonists before and after the advent of Techelec's new platform and the data it generates.

Before

We had a process-based, sequential series of steps whereby the operator would put on protective gear to draw a sample, take the sample to the lab, have the lab analyze the results on the chromatograph and then communicate the result back to the unit—at which point the reactor team would adjust the amount of acid being used to stay within the desired parameters. Meanwhile, the lab had to maintain protocols for the analysis, as did the maintenance, safety and health people responsible for the unit.

Now

All these discrete and sequential interactions have collapsed into what can be described as a collective "brain", whereby the refinery operators can make decisions on the fly by simply looking at the system's real-time data stream. Rather than being relegated to the roles of passive data recipients, the lab operators have become active problem solvers continuously interpreting what they see. They are connected to other resources within the plant (e.g., engineering, maintenance, safety and health) and can enlist their help as they see fit.

Techelec also has access to this new data stream, becoming smarter as more data is collected and bringing to O&G the fruits of this newfound intelligence. Over time, they start capturing additional data, expanding the scope of problems being solved. Together, the group co-develops the best solution at any given time, continuously improving, not only the use of the platform, but the platform itself.

In the end, our SAM orchestrated a complete rewiring of human interactions inside and outside the alkylation unit thanks to the data platform SAM's hand-picked team created together. The two firms made a commitment to each other and their relationship had grown stronger. Now they were family.

6   *The Family: Expand Value in All Directions*

Success breeds success. Once a SAM gets credited with the ability to solve one pesky problem for a customer, she inevitably gets invited to engage on other fronts. More engagement means more potential sales. Growth of the account comes in a variety of ways: from deepening the relationship from the first sale (as the supplier firm gets more and more data, it gets new ideas about services it can provide in their first field of success); from solving the same problem at other locations (the supplier deploys the solution at other places); or from being introduced by members of the customer team to other members of the customer's network with new problems. Over time, the cycle of co-creation applies to an ever-growing set of problems, owned by an expanding community of players on both sides who get more and more excited about their joint work. The relationship is nourished by a richer and richer set of data generated by a growing number of platforms linking the two firms, resulting into a constantly growing set of cross-company interactions and generating ever-growing value on both sides. This is co-creation nirvana.

In Techelec's case, the following is how value expanded after the first sale:

- Techelec was able to migrate the platform to ten other alkylation units at O&G, generating total sales in excess of $5 million.
- Impressed by Techelec's ability to develop an innovative process control system for its alkylation problem, O&G recently tasked Techelec with developing and marketing another process measurement solution the company developed in-house. This will produce yet another revenue layer without requiring the expensive R&D effort that is usually a cost of doing business.
- With the locations of all worldwide alkylation units of this type a matter of public record, Techelec has been able to sell its new and improved system to other oil and gas companies, including many with whom the company had no previous history.

7   The Value Co-Creation Map (VCM), a Key Tool for SAMs and Senior Buyers

One of the key roles of the SAM and the Senior Buyer is to develop an early view of the streams of value that can (and eventually will) be created between supplier and customer. A useful tool in that regard involves building a Value Co-Creation Map (or VCM for short). A VCM involves mapping out how five key components of the co-creation cycle identified in Chap. 2 (community, platforms, interactions, experience and value) feed into each other in a tree-like logic to tell the story of how the two companies will work together

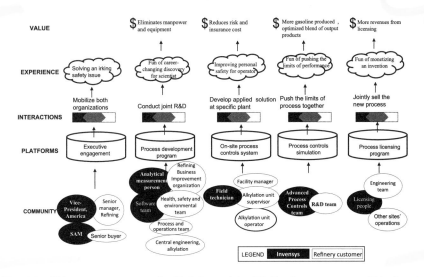

Fig. 3.2 Value co-creation map for Techelec and its O&G refinery customer. This chart is also available at http://www.eccpartnership.com/the-co-creation-edge.html

and what value they hope to generate from that joint work. It articulates what *community* needs to be assembled for the development of what *platform*, to produce what new *interactions* and create what type of *experience* for those members of the community, ultimately producing what type of *value* for the firms involved.

Figure 3.2 describes how Techelec's SAM constructed the co-creation program with his major counterparts at O&G, eventually putting in place the very successful program we described in the course of this chapter. The Value Co-Creation Map is often used at the outset of a co-creation project to facilitate the development of a shared agenda between both organizations. It is also often used to communicate in very synthesize fashion (typically one page) the story of the strategy the two companies are trying to put in place together. It is useful for the SAM and senior buyer to identify all the potential streams of value early on in the relationship-building process, but implementation is often staged over time since resources are often limited. By convention, the chronology of pursuit is represented on the VCM by locating the short-term value streams on the left of the chart and the longer-term ones on the right.

We will use the VCM tool throughout this book, using it as a summary of the cases presented in many subsequent chapters.

In this chapter, we illustrated, through the Techelec story, how the six steps of the strategic relationship-building process unfold over time and how the cycle of co-creation plays out at each step. In Chap. 4, we focus on the first of these six steps, and take a more detailed look at how to begin the co-creative journey.

CHAPTER 4

The Dream: Discover the Opportunity and Organize Internally

In Chaps. 2 and 3, we saw how the cycle of co-creation unfolds at each stage of the strategic relationship-building process. In this chapter, we start our more detailed exploration of each step, focusing on the first of our six stages: Discover the Opportunity and Organize Internally. In the human relationship metaphor, this constitutes the *dream* part, the moment where the supplier company imagines the collaboration it could develop with its customer, or vice-versa.

You may wonder why there is a need for this first stage. After all, isn't the best way to engage in a new relationship to just call up someone at the customer or supplier company and get going? Why is there a need for such a "co-creation inside" step? And isn't this type of co-creation with oneself a contradiction in terms?

The problem with attempting to enter into the relationship without spending time organizing internally is that you run the risk of your own team not being on the same page. Account teams, whether of the supplier or customer variety, are multi-functional and often involve multiple locations, which may result in diverging agendas. Engaging in co-creation frequently requires adding, over time, new members to the team that may not be familiar with the targeted partner firm. You do not want the members of your team to discover in front of the customer or supplier what the meeting is about and what co-creation involves. Beyond internal organization issues, you also need to have some ideas about what you want to engage your partner on. Co-creation is not improvisation. You need a pick-up line for your bar outing, and this requires researching the interests of the person you want to date. Knowing something about the other party will give you a chance to connect more meaningfully.

This front-end discovery of the potential customer, or supplier, is generally the most neglected phase of the six phases of our relationship-building process. SAMs and procurement people tend to be action- and contact-oriented: they prefer dancing to dreaming. Many are content to run a cursory Internet search through the company's annual report and take a quick look at some profiles of key people on LinkedIn, and off they go. This is a big mistake. The depth of engagement you will be able to create is proportional to the knowledge investment you make upfront. Unless you come up with a fresh, intriguing hypothesis about what to work on jointly, chances are you will either fail to engage the partner, or, at best, default to a fairly superficial encounter.

Each of the ten steps in our co-creation cycle takes on a particular form in this discovery phase. You will have to do the following:

1. Research the partner company and formulate the problem you want to tackle.
2. Mobilize the coalition inside your own firm and figure out who to pair them with on the partner side.
3. Host an internal workshop with your team.
4. Frame early questions and hypotheses on what to engage the partner on.
5. Envision the platform and process through which you will gather additional data with the help of the partner.
6. See what you can prove with the data you already have, and extrapolate from there.
7. Visualize the new interactions you want your company to have with the partner company.
8. Imagine what's in it for all parties, starting with your "work with" partner.
9. Formulate the value pitch for your "work with" partner.
10. Pitch the approach to your "work with" partner.

To show how this can be done, we turn to Becton Dickinson (BD), the global, New Jersey-based manufacturer of medical equipment and solutions.[1] BD enjoys a large market share in the syringes and needles business with hospitals and, back in the fall of 2012, was looking for its next avenue for growth. This turned out to be the co-creation effort described in this chapter.[2] Here, we specifically focus on the launch of the project, a phase centered around two internal workshop the Medical-Surgical Division conducted in Franklin Lakes, NJ, separated by about eight weeks of analytical work in late 2012, which eventually led to a successful multi-year, multi-customer program.

The head of the Injection Products business and his head of Marketing wanted to build a deeper relationship with its hospital customers. There are many types of syringes consumed by hospitals; Injection products are used, as the name indicates, to inject products into the body of patients fairly quickly, as opposed to infusion products that release the product more gradually in the body, as in chemotherapy sessions. Syringes designed to draw specimens such as blood from the human body are another type of device made by BD. All of these products have to meet stringent requirements set by regulators, such as the Food and Drug Administration in the US. There are sales people in each of those product divisions at BD, but the SAMs of the Medical-Surgical division handle the full line of these various products.

On the competitive front, SAMs were reporting that their job was getting tougher, as Chinese competitors were increasingly promoting their cheaper products on the global market, leading to price wars at many hospitals. The proverbial commoditization was setting in and the medical advice provided by the BD SAMs, while still valued, was increasingly weighed against the premium price charged by BD, potentially threatening the company's leadership position.

[1] See http://www.bd.com/medical-surgical/ for a description of Becton Dickinson's (BD) Medical Surgical Division.
[2] Ranjeet Banerjee, then Head of Injection Products at BD, and Mike Ferrara, then Head of Strategic Marketing at Injection Products, led the project described in this chapter. The larger project was originally described in a Harvard Business Review article co-authored by Francis Gouillart and Doug Billings, entitled *Community-Powered Problem Solving*, April 2013. In this chapter, we focus specifically on the early stages of the project and on the early development of the engagement plan created by the internal BD team.

1   Research the Partner Company and Formulate the Problem
You Want to Tackle

There is a chicken-and-egg nature to the determination of which comes first, the account you want to co-create with, or the problem you want to tackle. Ultimately, at the corporate level, you want your SAMs or senior buyers to develop a platform and engagement process that can be repeated across customers or suppliers (this is the new form taken by economies of scale in the co-creation world), but the best way to discover that is to go deep inside one account, try to figure out the exact nature of the issue at that particular account, demonstrate how one particular platform, or set of data, can help the supplier and customer jointly solve that problem, and only then see if the platform and engagement process can be reused across accounts on reasonably similar problems. In other words, and contrary to the teachings of many marketing gurus for the last 40 years, your company will learn more by engaging deeply with one account than by conducting multiple interviews to segment needs or quantify potential market size in each segment. The insights you gather from engaging deeply with *one* account will always beat the insights you generate from an exquisite (and expensive) study of the market of customer or suppliers. This is why individual SAMs and senior buyers are at the heart of co-creation.

But that's the corporate point of view. At the individual level, SAMs and senior buyers often ask themselves whether they should consider co-creation, and if so, which of their accounts they should pick. We suggest there are two criteria you should consider when deciding whether you want to engage in co-creation or not, one about yourself, the other about your account.

- First, ask yourself the question whether, as a SAM or senior buyer, you are psychologically prepared to enter into this co-creation dialog with your customer or supplier. Are you naturally curious about new approaches and willing to experiment with your customer? Do you like the notion of being a pioneer in a new approach, or are you more comfortable staying with the established customer or supplier relationship management process with its structured rewards for reaching quota or reducing spend, responding to request for proposals, or initiating them through more-or-less packaged solutions, using precise narratives, and rigorously tracking meetings and pipeline progress.

Can you see yourself picking up the phone and saying, "There is a big systemic problem that my company wants to tackle with you and we want to set up a joint discovery process leading to the development of a joint solution over time?"

If you think sticking your head out of the sales or procurement fox hole in this fashion is scary, you're right. It requires massive letting go on your part. Only do it if you have an aspiration to pioneer a new mode of relationship, transform your own role inside the company and withstand the inevitable pressure that will set in at some point. And this includes facing the dreaded question: How do I know that this will lead to sales or cost reduction within a reasonable time horizon? It will, but you will have to go through some anxious moments before you get there.

- Once you have established that you want to become a co-creator in your sales or procurement department, you will likely wonder which account to pick, assuming you handle multiple accounts. Pick the one where you have the most access, the one that is least secretive and where you believe there is some curiosity and openness to new approaches. Don't pick the heavily transaction-oriented, "everything-is-price-driven, "you're just a supplier" or "you're just a customer" company. Yes, you can sometimes transform some of those rigid transaction cultures in the long run, but only at the end of a long journey, so don't start there.

Do not pick the biggest of your accounts either. It's better to start "off-Broadway" to learn how to do it right. There will be plenty of times to attack larger accounts later on. It's OK to pick friendlier territories for your maiden voyage. Yes, accounts where you have weaker relationships, or no relationship at all, will become important over time, do not start there. Start with your friends, learn how co-creation works, and once you've gained self-confidence, venture into more hazardous terrains, armed with your new knowledge.

At BD, each SAM handles a limited number of hospitals, sometimes only one for particularly large accounts. The SAM's job is to address the needle and syringes needs of these hospitals. Each hospital account typically comprises one or more big central downtown facilities and a scattered network of satellite offices run by affiliated doctors. The proliferation of these satellite offices is a relatively recent phenomenon, the result of the massive land grab that is taking place with hospitals acquiring more and more independent doctors' practices and putting them on their payroll to feed their hospital facilities[3] (this is the process euphemistically described as "referring patients"). The prevailing wisdom is that most hospitals need to bulk up to survive the Darwinian healthcare consolidation game. In late 2012, there was a noticeable post-merger indigestion at many hospitals, a sense that things were no longer fully in control as a result of this rapid throwing together of heterogeneous bedfellows inside the newly formed doctors' networks.

Some of the more adventurous SAMs immediately saw that this might constitute an opportunity for BD. They could see the proliferation of care places had resulted in more hospital locations consuming medical-surgical products. The multiplication of delivery places made their job (and the job of BD's distributors) more complex, but they also noticed it was even harder for the hospital's central procurement and supply chain staff to gain and maintain control over the practices of these individual offices. In the word of one of the supply chain managers at a medium-sized New Jersey hospital, "we have a mess on our hands."

One of the symptoms of this acquisition spree had been the development of infections resulting from poor needle practices. Needle incidents are bad enough since they hurt patients, but to (literally) add insult to injury, they increase the count of Hospital-Acquired Infections (HAI), a published statistic on hospitals scorecards, leading to a potentially bad grade on an important metric. This bad grade, in turn, hurts the hospitals' reimbursement rate paid by private and government insurance programs. The SAMs knew infections in remote offices were rapidly becoming a big issue. They could see the pain in the eyes of their "work with" customers in procurement and supply chain. They could read about the growing concern over hepatitis B or AIDS and knew that bad injection practices were a potential culprit.[4] There were alarming stories of infection-caused epidemics in emerging countries such as

---

[3] See for example the Wall Street Journal article entitled *Healthcare Providers, Insurers Supersize*, September 2015, available at http://www.wsj.com/articles/health-care-providers-insurers-supersize-1442850400.

[4] See for example USA Today article entitled *Dirty Medical Needles Put Tens of Thousands at Risk in USA*, March 6, 2013, available at http://www.usatoday.com/story/news/nation/2012/12/26/infections-needles-mrsa-hospitals/1780335/.

India, but even the most prestigious American or Western European health-care institutions were not spared the ignominy of seeing their name associated with serious infection issues.

Buoyed by this discovery, and encouraged by their division leadership and the head of the SAM program, several SAMs decided they had to understand the expansion strategy of their hospital account and its consequences on operations. They discovered how many acquisitions had already taken place in their account, how many more were planned, and who their hospital cus-tomer might try to acquire next. Each acquisition of doctors' practice became an opportunity to gain share for BD. If the prevention of infection through good injection practices was to become the centerpiece of the SAM program, they needed to research the HAI track record of each account from public health records and other sources. They then had to determine where these infections had originated within the hospital. Looking for published articles on the problem, they had to ascertain what the post-merger acquisition pro-cess looked like at those large hospital chains: Who was in charge, and how was the infection prevention issue being handled as facilities were consoli-dated? Was there a central group handling the issue? Was it left to each loca-tion's initiative? And how could BD play a role in addressing the problem?

The good news for the SAMs was that there was a precedent for BD taking a leadership role in the safe injection area. Many years earlier, BD had spear-headed a similar industry-wide initiative by helping to develop the standards and protocols that big hospital facilities utilized to control for infections in their central facility. BD had pretty much written the book on the topic, unleashing many years of steady growth in revenues and profitability. But creating standards for big downtown hospitals with concentrated personnel and quality control staff on-site was one thing. Could they do the same for remote doctors' offices in the network of those large hospital chains?

At a SAM meeting of the Medical Surgical division in December 2012, two BD SAMs initially volunteered to try the new co-creation approach focused on the safe injection hypothesis. The leaders of the Injection prod-ucts business made the corporate push for the new co-creation approach, but it took for two individual SAMs to put their hand up and say, "I'm willing to try this." Not coincidentally, they were not handling the largest accounts of the firm, but two mid-sized hospital accounts in the Northeastern United States. Neither hospital was representative of the major big-city accounts of the firm, but they thought this was something new and fresh they could bring to their customers and say, "We think we should address the infection issue at the systemic level and we will figure it out together." They became BD's co-creation pioneers.

2 Mobilize the Internal Coalition and Figure Out Who to Pair Them with on the Partner Side

Since co-creation involves a many-to-many dialog between supplier and customer, the second task of the SAM or senior manager is to assemble the "many" within your own company. Not surprisingly, building the coalition inside one's own firm often proves as difficult as assembling it on the partner's side. Co-creation inside can be as hard as co-creation outside.

To identify the right community of players that you need both inside and outside your company, start with the problem you are trying to tackle and what you know about the co-creation partner you have picked. Think about it in "chunks"; do not build the world's largest spaghetti chart where everybody is connected to everybody, but try to identify sub-communities of people who belong together to discuss specific subsets of the larger problem you want to tackle. Think of it as community segmentation, or community pairing. As you will rapidly discover, there is an art to it, because the effectiveness of each sub-group will be a function of the personal chemistry that develops between people. This is basically the old "face-off plan" advocated by many selling methodologies, except that the sub-groups identified will do a lot more than sell each other or negotiate; they will engage in the joint generation of data to solve problems in common, a very different purpose.

Figure 4.1 describes five generic sub-communities that SAMs and senior procurement people will typically have to engage over time for large transformational projects. It will take some time for the various sub-communities to get started; don't get discouraged if you get only one or two of these groups going in the early stages. Sales (led by the SAM) and procurement (led by the senior buyer) typically engage with each other first since it is their role. The second sub-community involves mobilizing the technical support functions of the supplier and the operations group of the customer, with the goal of improving process efficiency at the customer. The third sub-community has the product development, or R&D group of the supplier, work with functional leadership on the customer side that are responsible for the use of the new products or services in developing new applications for existing products, or outright new products or services. The fourth sub-community mobilizes the functions responsible for the relationship with the larger eco-system of the supplier and the buyer, such as Chief Sustainability Officers, Public Relations Officers, Political Affairs or Community Relationship lead-ers, whose agenda is to not only change the relationship between supplier and customer, but also the larger relationship with their ecosystem's members. The fifth and final sub-community involves engaging C-level executives on both sides. This happens in the most ambitious form of co-creation, when supplier and customer attempt to create a new business model of strategic importance to both firms, sometimes also transforming the larger industry they participate in.

Using the template from Fig. 4.1, here are the five specific sub-communities the BD team envisioned engaging at the first discovery workshop they held.

- *BD Strategic Account Managers with Senior Buyers at hospital chain*: The *SAM* and the *senior procurement person* will constitute the core of the engagement team. This will be the classic sales-procurement or procurement-to-sales tandem.

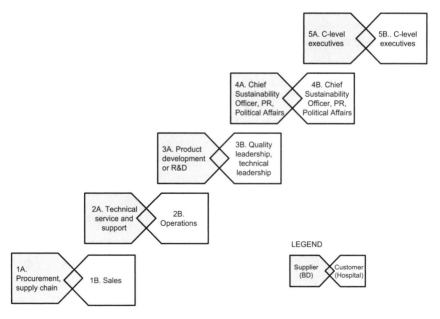

Fig. 4.1 Five sub-communities SAMs and senior buyers will typically have to engage. This chart is also available at http://www.eccpartnership.com/the-co-creation-edge.html

- BD SAMs will pair up with the senior procurement person and the supply chain manager at the two hospitals, and together, they will constitute the anchor of the relationship.
- *BD Field Technical People and Hospital Operations*: Many problems will require that we add *operations people* who can speak to service and supply chain issues on both sides if the issue we want to tackle involves any form of operational improvement, or efficiency-driven program. This will involve *customer service and field technical people* on the BD side, and *plant or field service people* on the hospital side.
  - For our BD SAMs, the owner of the safe injection issue will be the Infectious Disease Leader (who worries about safety for patients) and the Occupational Health Leader (who worries about the health of healthcare workers in the hospital). On the BD side, the Medical Affairs and Regulatory Managers will be their natural face-off point. The Infectious Disease and Occupational Safety Leaders at the hospitals are known to our two SAMs, but they have largely been off-limits to them as BD has been thought to be "a vendor of quality medical devices", which does not warrant particular attention on their part. Back at headquarters, BD's Medical Affairs and Compliance managers know they can bring a lot of value to those hospitals, from their research and experience of infection issues, including clinical trials, but we will need to figure out how to give them access to the hospital clinical leaders. It will take a bit of horse-trading on the part of our two SAMs to convince the Medical Affairs and Regulatory departments to support our project, but the combination of some personal contacts and the inherent attraction for staff people in becoming involved in a sales effort will eventually produce the desired result.
- *BD Research and Development with Clinical and Medical Leaders at the hospital chain*: Still broadening the scope of the engagement, our community will need to involve our *R&D, or Product Development* people, since we think the effort will require the development of new products or services. This may, in turn, require the involvement of some of the hospital chain's functional leaders, such as managers in their *Legal, Compliance, Medical Affairs, or Sustainability* departments.
  - Our SAMs know that involving product development people at the outset represents a long shot, as headquarter engineers are naturally

suspicious of any value coming from hospital users, given the highly technical and regulated nature of the product. Sure enough, BD's R&D people were indeed quite busy meeting their product launch deadlines and initially declined involvement in the first effort, but they joined in later, once the program became more established, using the co-creation engagement process to validate their design with users and using the excitement of their customers to secure the funding resources for their favorite project.

- *Managers of BD's ecosystem and Managers of the hospital chain's ecosystem*: Moving into more and more ambitious territory will require the involvement of some of our *suppliers and partners*, given that the problem we want to tackle involves critical supplies or materials and the provision of complex IT tools that only external IT suppliers can provide. We also expect that on the customer side the hospital chain, we may have to call on its *customers' customers*, such as the cities or large companies they serve.

  - Our BD SAMs realized early on that they would need some solid IT capability to develop the data platforms required to support the tracking of infection issues at their hospitals and the development of any kind of predictive modeling of incidents, eventually leading to the development of a prevention approach to eliminate those incidents in the first place. The CIO of the Medical-Surgical Division was a creative, forward-looking manager who had developed a close relationship with Microsoft Healthcare. Together, they had been looking for a first field of application for the new cloud business within BD, and the two SAMs offered them, on a platter, a "proof-of-concept" opportunity.

- *Senior Management of BD working with Executives at the hospital chain*: Ultimately, our co-creation effort requires the involvement of the *C suite for both BD and the hospital chain*. Our *CFO* will have to get involved because the magnitude of the co-creation will have an impact on the overall financials of the firm. Our *CIO and CTO will* also have to become involved, given the key role of technology and data in the co-creation approach. We anticipate that our *CEO* will have to become engaged if our program reaches the transformational level we aspire to.

- At BD, the leadership of the Injection Products Division was involved from day one, which provided a lot of air cover for our two BD SAMs. Initially, there was no access to the C suite on the hospital side, but our two SAMs established that as their goal: to reach this highest level at some point.

Of course, as a SAM or senior buyer, you should not expect to reach these higher spheres of management right away, but you should use the discovery phase of the relationship-building process to articulate the various layers of engagement you will have to go through.

3   Host an Internal Workshop with Your Team

Once you have your community lineup figured out on both sides, convene an internal workshop with your team. The objective of the workshop should be to arrive at the pitch your company will have for the partner firm. This will require answering the ten questions of the co-creation cycle to the best of your ability, from framing the problem you want to tackle, all the way to identifying the value created for both parties and developing a joint transformation agenda.

Of course, your hypotheses will be crude, ill-formed, or even wrong, at such an early stage in the game (there is only so much you can glean from Internet searches and public information), but the workshop will serve a dual purpose. First, it will give your future partner the confidence that you have done your homework and have truly thought about their business, even though you may turn out to be wrong about some of the issues or opportunities you've identified (they'll straighten you out if they think you've earned the right to engage with them). Second, your team will have gone through the intellectual gymnastics of co-creation (for example, your team will see how the ten-step model works), which will allow them to move from passive student to active teacher in the workshop with the customer in phase two of the relationship-building process.

At BD, the first workshop lasted one day and included about 15 people, including two SAMs and the head of the SAM program, in addition to selected resources from Medical Affairs, Compliance, Sustainability, Finance and IT. The workshop started with the two leaders laying out a possible vision for the Injection Products Division, including the role that a possible Safe Injection co-creation approach might take. The head of the business was both a humanist and a businessman, and he provided an ethical and a capitalistic motivation for engaging with their hospital customers in a new way. The head of Marketing took on the more analytical role and offered the process of co-creation they might have to go through to get to the desired vision of a safe injection in remote doctors' offices.

There were two types of reactions. On the positive side, participants liked the notion of doing something in their professional life they would feel proud about and could share with their families and friends. On the concern side, the ability to convert this approach into sales dollars felt so uncertain and distant that some thought it quite risky. The two SAMs were skeptical, underlining that their life was one of hitting monthly sales quota to feed the public company quarterly financials, and there was little time to embark on something this long-term and fuzzy. There was also a proliferation of initiatives competing for resources, and the co-creation effort was only one of them. Why undertake this one when there were so many "low-hanging fruit" sales opportunities around?

The two leaders off the business chose not to force the issue, but invited the group to go through the process for the one-day workshop, discover what it entails, and then decide over the course of the next few weeks whether to embark on it.

4   Frame Early Questions and Hypotheses on What to Engage the Partner on

At the workshop, after identifying the sub-communities that might engage in the various streams of co-creation, frame the questions you think need to be answered. Frame each question in as analytical fashion as possible, centering on one or two variables you intend to measure, and wherever possible, try to anticipate correlation between variables (hypothesize what drives what).

Most companies are missing this step and have never developed a process that helps them frame the right questions. The question cannot simply be "how can I sell more?" for the SAM, and "how can I reduce spend" for the senior buyer. Co-creation is the art of asking the five or ten questions that precede this "selling more" or "spending less" question. What makes truly great SAMs or senior buyers is their ability to devise the series of questions that lead to answers that can produce the desired result of solving a big problem, resulting in huge sales or massive cost reductions. Some people liken this process to crossing a river by jumping from stone to stone, hoping that each of them is stable, or strong enough, to support the weight of the person attempting to cross.

At this stage, many questions will inevitably be open and not led by any particular hypothesis. This is a perfectly fine way to go, particularly in a Big Data world where correlations sometimes reveal themselves only after collecting lots of data in the hope of discovering predictive patterns over time, as the data set grows. In some cases, the outcome may prove to be improvable as a result of some action you take, and, in other cases, you may not find any meaningful correlation and will have wasted your time and effort. This is the price you pay. On the other hand, if you have some *a priori* idea about a possible correlation between two variables, your work will be greatly facilitated since you know exactly what data to collect. The latter approach is the more traditional deterministic or scientific approach where you hypothesize causes and effects *a priori* and test the causal relationship. The former is what the new world of Big Data allows, with all its glorious uncertainty: collect first, figure out the correlation later. If you, as a SAM or senior buyer, become an evangelist of co-creation, be prepared to explain the difference between both approaches at every corner, and prepare yourself for a fight with the more traditional business methodologists who will sarcastically argue with you that "if you don't know where you're going, every road will lead you there".

At BD, the group came up with some of the following questions at the workshop:

For the Operations stream of co-creation centered on the Infectious Disease and Occupancy Health Leaders on the hospital side:

1. Can we get fewer needle prick incidents for the targeted hospitals?
2. Can we reduce the hospitals overall injection system costs?
3. Will this produce more business for BD?

Product development

4. Can a better needle design further reduce the number of needle pricks?
5. Can we further reduce the injection system cost for the hospital?
6. Will this help BD develop better products and we will sell more of them?

Sustainability

7. Can we reduce the environmental footprint of the hospital?
8. Can we reduce the safety risk posed by the disposal of our needles?
9. Can our sustainability service differentiate us in the mind of key decision-makers at the hospital?

Financial

10. Can we help hospitals reduce their insurance payment?
11. Can we capture some of the premium reductions created for the hospital as a fee?

Notice three things about those questions: First, they are all formulated in such a fashion that they contain at least one measurable element. Avoid questions that are loose and qualitative, since they cannot be tested through data. Good SAMs and senior buyers are analytically obsessed about the wording of those questions.

Second, most variables were not being measured by either BD or the hospital chain (total injection costs, for example, was a new concept). It is OK to devise new measures thought to be relevant to the issue you are trying to solve. As a general rule of thumb, you should try to have 50% of the measures you devise that already exist, and 50% can be new measures you will develop with your partner.

Thirdly, notice how relatively crude these questions and associated measures are. The hypotheses at this stage do not have to be well formed (and how could they be, since the company has not yet engaged its partner and is, therefore, lacking a lot of knowledge?), but they have to define a general area of investigation that your partner will further refine with you, something akin to hacking at a block of granite that two sculptors (supplier and customer) will relentlessly chisel together over the next few months.

5 Envision the Platform and Process Through Which You Will Gather Additional Data with the Help of the Partner

Now that you've laid out the questions you want to answer, and the metrics you need to capture on the way to answering those questions, you need a practical way to gather that data. This requires two things: a view of the data-generating platform from a content standpoint, and a process through which you will engage the other party in co-developing that platform (or at least tolerate the intrusion that it will represent for them if you bring the platform to them).

Think of the platform as the electronic connector that links your two firms, allowing some joint analysis of the data it generates. This data collection effort is often done manually the first time around (one has to start somewhere and this is where the IT specifications for the platform will come from, typically in the first two or three projects where you engage in co-creation with pioneering customers or suppliers), but given the global scope of business-to-business relationships, the platform will need to scale quickly after that, which requires some form of electronic intermediation. The platform is the backbone of co-creation, so the first sale you will have to make to your partner is on the idea of the platform itself. If your partner accepts the idea of installing a platform (or, better yet, co-developing it with you), this is a strong indication that strong sales (for the SAM) or significant cost reduction opportunities (for the senior buyer) will follow.

In some cases, the platform connecting the two businesses already exists, at least in partial form, providing a foundation that can be built on. More and more data feeds already exist between companies (such as Electronic Data Interchange and web-based ordering interfaces), and many products already carry some form of "sensing" ability relaying data back to both companies (most cars and manufacturing machines, for example, capture live data that is accessible to both the original equipment manufacturer and the user). In other cases, you will have to develop a new platform out of whole cloth (or whole silicon).

The other item you need to conceptualize at this stage is the live process of engagement that allows you to develop and "drop" the data platform that will become the nervous system of the relationship. Allowing someone, a supplier of customer, to install a permanent data feed inside your operation requires a lot of trust, and that trust must be earned through human blood and sweat, which means organizing meetings, workshops, and intense joint development mini-projects to create consensus on what the platform should look like and what its benefits are for both parties. The problem is that at this stage of the co-creation process, you do not have access to the other party, and you are largely guessing at what is acceptable or desirable to them: where the platform development effort will fit in their IT priorities, whether they will have the resources to at least work with you on developing the specifications, or better yet participate in the development, or whether they will be willing to contribute to the financing of the platform. You don't know the response to any of those questions, but you have to present them with an opening picture of what this engagement process could look like and engage in the conversation. The more you've thought about it, the less likely it is that you will be turned down outright.

At BD, our two SAMs worked with the internal group that was assembled at the workshop and devised a simple four-step process, with the first two steps coming before the sale and the next two after the sale:

- They envisioned a brief "Identify" (step 1) and "Improve" (step 2) phase of work, which would be conducted by a newly formed, dedicated, four-member SWAT team under the leadership of the SAM. They imagined the effort might last two or three weeks and would be financed by BD as part of its selling cost. The idea was to conduct an analytical blitz that would generate immediate opportunities for improvement ("quick hits") and provide the business case for the larger effort (with a "this project pays for itself" logic). Most importantly, it allowed BD to make the case for laying out the long-term data platforms to allow both companies to continue making progress long after the initial analytical blitz, generating a continuous flow of new insights from the data. In other words, the short-term benefits would create the credibility for the promise that more insights are forthcoming if you allow us to install the data platform in your operation.
- The two subsequent phases after the sale were conceptualized as Sustain (phase 3) and Innovate (phase 4). The Sustain phase allowed both companies to analyze new patters of incidents and take preventive measures in offices, or with personnel known to be incident-prone. In the Innovation phase, they envisioned developing some predictive models, allowing both companies to anticipate incidents before they occurred, for example, detecting ordering patterns showing that less attention was being paid to safety, or personnel ratios suggesting that cost compression might lead to problems at a later stage.

The more specific you can be about the platforms you envision, the better, but there is, of course a great deal you still have to learn about the partner. The typical platform design at stage one of the relationship-building process is mostly conceptual, highlighting five to ten modules, or mini-platforms, you think might be helpful, with a high-level description of the content of each of them and how they will contribute to answering the questions that were posed earlier.

At BD, the team identified three platforms it would develop during the Identify and Improve SWAT phases:

1. Tools and checklist to conduct a diagnostic of the hospital's injection effectiveness: This would give the central Infection Disease staff a framework to analyze where the hospital is at in terms of its best practices.
2. End-to-end injection process assessment: This platform would focus on the physical process of injection and its safety.
3. Customized safety assurance roadmap: This would represent the "to be" state of where the hospital might want to go in the future.

It envisioned developing five more platforms in the Sustain-and-Improve phase, after the sale of the project.

4. BD device optimization: This would link the BD product development people with actual users in some fashion.
5. Knowledge Management Center: This platform would have a set of resources originally provided by BD for use by hospital staff, and would become enriched over time through the collective learnings of the hospital community working on injection safety.
6. eLearning Training Modules: The group envisioned packaged best practice modules that would be developed in the future and marketed by a third-party company.
7. Sustainability Lifecycle Simulator: They conceptualized a tool that would simulate how plastic used syringes and needles could be recycled as large plastic containers through which the hazardous waste could be disposed (closed loop).
8. Accreditation Support and Insurance Risk: They sketched out a model hypothesizing how the accumulation of safe injection improvements could be used by the hospital CFO to model the resulting reduction in risk, and justify a renegotiation of insurance premium for the hospital.

The platform ideas were crude and the process of engagement fairly conceptual, but our two SAMs now had a straw model they could show their counterpart in procurement and supply chain at the hospitals.

6 See What You Can Prove with the Data You Already Have, and Extrapolate from There

Unless you're entering into a brand new relationship, you should already have some relevant data at your disposal. As a SAM, you may already be selling into the account, although not as much as you might like. As a senior buyer, you may already be purchasing from the supplier you want to grow. You may think the customer already knows what he buys and the supplier knows what he spends, since they are on the other side of your company's transaction. Surprisingly, we repeatedly find this is, at best, partially true, and sometimes not true at all. IT systems are often disjointed or incomplete, and companies often do not spend the time required to analyze their sales, or their spend, and giving them feedback on what they buy or sell is a cheap way of adding value quickly, while offering a glimpse into additional insights likely to emerge once a new platform connects the two firms. Benchmark data from other customers or suppliers (properly sanitized) can also quickly bring analytical value to the discussion and act as a metaphor for bigger and better value to come.

The two BD SAMs hypothesized at the workshop that giving their two hospital accounts a view of the purchases made by their doctors across their networks (and particularly their "new" doctors from recent acquisitions) represented value in itself. Needles and syringes range from the cheap, unsophisticated variety to the highest quality type, and the price differential is driven, among other things, by the amount of safe injection quality that is "baked" into the device. By providing Infectious Disease and Occupational Health Leaders with an overview of who was buying what in their network, they were effectively suggesting to them that some offices invested more than others in injection safety, an analysis which provided a first snapshot of which offices were emphasizing safety, and which might have it as a lesser priority. This gave Infectious Disease Leaders some indication of where they should direct their efforts. It also made credible the two SAMs' assertion that "there are plenty more insights to come where this came from".

7 Visualize the New Interactions You Want Your Company to Have with the Partner Company

Most SAMs and senior buyers have participated at some point in their life in reengineering, Six Sigma quality or Lean efforts. As a result, they tend to equate interaction with process, thus when invited to think about interactions with their customer or supplier, they automatically move into a reengineering mode and try to "fix" some broken process. This is not what we are talking about here. Fixing broken processes is clearly a good thing to do, but co-creation seeks *new* connections that never existed before. One way of thinking about those interactions is to view them as "missing", i.e., they represent a missing link that helps members of the supplier-customer community solving new problems. The reason these missing interactions are important is that they represent an opportunity to drop an engagement platform between the disconnected parties and begin generating a flow of new data between them, which will lead to generating new insights and solving new problems.

There are two basic ways of imagining new interactions. One is to build an "as is" interaction map that identifies, on one dimension, all the existing players and on the other dimension, what interactions they have with each other today (you have to build separate maps for each broad functional areas to avoid making it unwieldy), then do one of three things:

- Imagine new interactions between the existing players you have identified,
- Or introduce new players that might become involved and expand the field of interactions,
- Or do both at once, i.e., introduce new players doing new things.

The other way to proceed is to not constrain yourself with existing interactions at all, and start with a representation of the community of stakeholders on both sides, and simply draw new connections between them in a game of "connect the dots".

The first approach will typically yield good operational results in that the SAM or procurement team will get excited about mapping their existing field of interactions and easily imagine new ways of expanding those interactions beyond what exists. The suggestions coming out of this approach are often practical, because they are rooted in the knowledge of what people do every day. The downside is that starting with what exists can lead to more incremental ideas than imagining brand new connections linking disjointed players, unencumbered by the weight of today's reality, which can lead to more strategic breakthroughs. And of course, the downside of the free-thinking approach is that it can become theoretical and practically un-implementable.

The BD SAMs, coached by the Director of Marketing, became heavy users of interaction maps. They created about ten of them for Injection Products (and many more later on, when the effort broadened beyond Injection products to the entire Medical-Surgical Division), taking the perspective of individual people, either on the hospital chain side, or on the BD side. By definition, an interaction map centers on the perspective of one particular player, say, the Infection Disease Leader at the hospital, and looks at the world from her perspective: who does she interact with within the hospital network, and who does she work on the BD side? Our two SAMs noticed that the Infection Disease Leader had no real interaction with individual doctors and nurses in remote offices around safety performance. There were no reports flowing back and forth between individual offices and the "Safety Central" function at headquarters managed by the Infectious Disease Leader. This missing interaction around the reporting of safety incidents, as identified during the interaction mapping exercise at the very first internal workshop, became the foundation for the incident reporting platform later on in the effort.

Interaction maps can be made into living documents. The first interaction maps drawn by BD purely internally were sometimes quite naïve in their attempt at describing what was taking place in the hospital chain, but they proved effective conversation openers for working sessions with the hospital staff later on. Some were greeted by outright hilarity ("is this really what you guys think is going on within our walls?"), but rapidly turned into constructive information-sharing ("this is what is really going on that you don't see"). In other words, interaction maps are an effective tool to structure dialog between both firms, with the first draft done by the internal BD team in the Discovery Phase acting as foundation for subsequent discussions.

8   Imagine What's in It for All Parties, Starting with Your "Work with" Partner

Businesses, both yours and the one of your customer or supplier partner, are made of people who will be naturally skeptical of your aspiration to engage with them. There has to be something intensely personal for anybody to engage in co-creation with you and overcome the natural aversion that most of us have toward risk, or taking on more work. There has to be an objective win or "business case" for both businesses (we'll get into that in the value section next), but long before that, your role is to generate a personal win for anybody who engages with you, starting with the person you have most immediate access to, your "work with" partner. What's in it for him? Why would he help you? What is it that will change the day-to-day experience your partner will have of his work?

As a SAM or senior buyer, you should have no qualms about personalizing the corporate agenda in this fashion. There is nothing shameful, or manipulative, about trying to feed into the personal agenda of your counterpart at the partner firm, as long as the personal agenda is in congruence with the corporate agenda of both firms. Great teams are made of individuals who all have a personal agenda (this is particularly true of their star players), but the role of the coach is to channel the personal agendas of these players into a collective team agenda that leads the team to win. The same is true for the SAM or senior buyer. Your role is to assemble an "experience network" that creates a personal win for all stakeholders in your company and the partner company, such that it ultimately creates corporate value for both companies.

At BD, our two SAMs formulated the following value proposition for their immediate counterparts at the hospital: "we'll make you into a rock star". They imagined delivering that message to both the senior buyer and the supply chain manager for needles and syringes they worked with. They practiced (and later actually conducted) the conversation where they would sell their "work with" partners on the promise of earning greater respect from the medical staff at the hospital by bringing new tools and platforms developed by BD that would improve the experience of the Infectious Disease and Occupational Health people through data. They highlighted how this would boost the supply chain people's credibility and help them advance their career. It also gave them the pitch to the Infectious Disease Leader: "through the data that BD will provide you with, you will now be able to do a great job and sleep at night".

9 Formulate the Corporate Value Pitch for Your "Work with" Partner

Ultimately, co-creation needs to entail a win for both companies, as measured in their bottom line. Just as we identified five generic "sub-communities" earlier in this chapter, there are generally five generic layers of value resulting from co-creation efforts, as shown in Fig. 4.2.

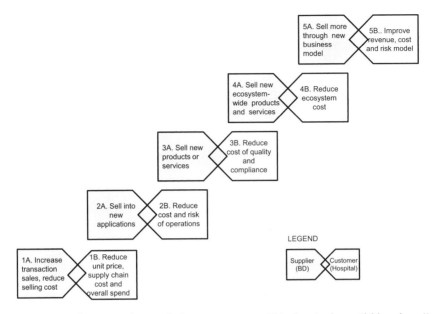

Fig. 4.2 The five generic layers of value in co-creation. This chart is also available at http://www.eccpartnership.com/the-co-creation-edge.html

1. Reduced procurement costs (for the customer) and selling costs (for the buyer), and reduced supply chain costs on both sides, stemming from moving away from a hard-nosed, transaction-intensive negotiation process and replacing it with a more transparent and integrated order-to-cash process:

   - The BD SAMs hypothesized that both sides would save money if the procurement and sales processes were made more transparent to each other, with better communication of volume forecasts and longer-term commitment of volume by the hospital chain, with lower per unit prices from BD based on greater cost predictability on some products, and reduction of inventory and transport costs coming from sharing supply chain data across both companies.

2. Increased sales for the supplier as a result of improving operations at the customer level, and reduction of cost and risk at the customer:

   - The BD SAMs hypothesized that if they could equip the Infectious Disease and Occupational Health Leaders with the right data about injection safety, BD sales would be rewarded through an increase in its market share with the hospital chain. There was some apprehension about that, given that the data they intended to provide was not directly part of the product being sold (unlike, say, a heart-monitoring device where the platform is embedded into the product), but they imagined they would discuss the *quid pro quo* at the outset of the relationship.

3. Reduced operating costs on the customer side coming from the supplier designing next-generation products that optimize use of the product in the customer's operations, resulting in sales of new products for the supplier:

   • At BD, the SAMs envisioned that product developers, by engaging directly with nurses and doctors, would be able to come up with new products or product utilization processes that would be highly successful commercially. They imagined that the healthcare workers that had worked with the designers would act as a surrogate sales force for future products, helping their commercialization.

4. Increased sales of products and services for the supplier, resulting from reducing the cradle-to-grave costs of using the supplier product not only at the customer level, but also across an expanded ecosystem of players upstream or downstream from the supplier-customer tandem:

   • At BD, the SAMs figured that if the company took responsibility for the disposal of used needles and syringes and partnered with waste management companies, municipalities and health regulators, it would generate new sources of revenues for the firm, while allowing the hospitals to reduce their waste management costs. They also envisioned that partnering with waste management companies, municipalities and health regulators would generate new sales leads because of the breadth of service offering created, thereby allowing a clear strategic differentiation vs. commodity needle suppliers.

5. Development of a new business model that creates new revenue sources for the customer and a sweeping reduction in cost, investment or risk for the customer:

- At BD, the SAMs imagined with the group that if they could demonstrate significant operational improvement in injection safety at their hospital account through the operational, product design and sustainability platforms they had put in place, they would be in a position to go to the CFO of those hospitals and say, "We think we have reduced your risk dramatically and would like to discuss how we can jointly go to your insurance company and jointly negotiate a new contract with them that results in a savings we would share in."

10   Pitch the Approach to Your "Work with" Partner

The ultimate goal of this first discovery phase, as you recall, is to develop the narrative you will use in your pitch to your "work with" partner at the customer or supplier firm. This narrative is the story built through the previous nine steps, and culminating in this tenth step.

Here is the pitch developed by the two SAMs at BD.

1. PROBLEM: Let's tackle the injection safety issue together
2. COMMUNITY: You, in procurement and supply chain, and I, in sales, have been working together for a while. I'd like to introduce you to a team of new players that know a lot about injection safety.
3. HUMAN ENGAGEMENT PLATFORM: Let's put a joint SWAT team together to show the art of the possible in your hospital and blitz the injection safety problem in three or four weeks.
4. OPPORTUNITIES: Together, we want to explore whether we can reduce the number of needle sticks and lower your injection system costs.
5. DATA PLATFORM: We, the supplier, will invest in a tablet-based system that brings best practices and gives you actual data on where your vulnerabilities lie.
6. INSIGHTS: looking at your needle purchase data, we already know where some of the problem areas are likely to be.
7. INTERACTIONS: We will give your Infectious Disease and Occupational Health Leaders the ability to show doctors and nurses in remote offices how to avoid infection problems.

8. NEW EXPERIENCES: We will make you into a rock star. This will earn you consideration from the clinical staff at the hospital.

9. VALUE: over time, the reduction of injection safety incidents will reduce your system cost, and will draw the attention of your C suite.

Both SAMs took this narrative to their hospital procurement and supply chain partners and successfully sold them on what became a multi-year program. Not everything they initially hypothesized materialized in the actual project when actual hospitals became involved, but the initial workshop described in this chapter provided the blueprint for about 70% of the actual co-creation program that developed over the next few years. The program has now blossomed way beyond the original two hospitals and has spread widely across multiple care providers in the US and abroad. The program has also expanded beyond Injection products to the full line of devices made by the Medical-Surgical Division of BD.[5]

In this chapter, we concentrated on the first step in the six steps we call Discover the Opportunity and Organize Internally. We likened it to the Dream portion in the building of a human relationship. It culminates with reaching out to the person or people you know in the partner organization and convincing them to take a personal risks and give you access to the rest of the organization to pitch the co-creation approach to a larger audience. If you manage to make this sale, the next question is to devise what happens next. This is the task we turn to in the next chapter: Envision the Value and Assemble a Joint Team.

---

[5] Source: interviews of Ranjeet Banerjee and Mike Ferrara at BD.

CHAPTER 5

The Dance: Envision the Value and Assemble a Joint Team

Y ou now have a concept of the value that can be created between the two firms and you have established contact with the other party. In this chapter, we discuss how to engage with each other in practical fashion and jointly envision the value that can be created. The principal focus of this stage is to get organized across both firms and assemble a joint team that will pursue the opportunities that have been identified.

Figuring out how to engage with each other is not a trivial point. The way in which you position this first encounter will make a big difference later on. The more the other party understands what you have in mind, the larger the scope of the co-creation you will ultimately produce. In our human relationship metaphor, this is the equivalent of the dance between the two partners. The invitation to the dance can be tentative, the dance itself a bit awkward, but the process will reveal whether there is a natural attraction between the partners. In all cases, you will not know until you try, so get on with it.

In many ways, you will be reproducing in this step what you have already done internally in the previous step. The main difference is that you are now truly engaging live with the other party, rather than merely speculating internally on how the other party will react. You will find the reality to be quite different from what you had envisioned, but will have the advantage of being prepared for all eventualities. Don't be turned off if your partner's reactions are not what you expected, just try to adapt in real time to what you encounter. The best relationships do not originate with a killer formulation of the problem you conceive and sell to your partner: they come from an imperfect problem formulation you create, which your partner morphs beyond recognition to make it his own.

Here is how the ten phases of the co-creation cycle play out in this second step of the relationship-building cycle:

1. Adapt your problem formulation to what the other party wants to see addressed.
2. Create a face-off plan for each stream of work you design and recruit the team members needed for the effort on both sides.
3. Get the team mobilized and aligned on the formulation of the problem.
4. Agree on the specific hypotheses you want to tackle.
5. Envision the platform and process through which you will gather the needed data.
6. Experiment with the new platform and see what the data shows.
7. Design the new process of interaction, including negotiation, in the new order.
8. Unleash a current of personal empathy between key players.
9. Identify early value created and create a buzz around it.
10. Envision how the initial platform can be expanded to create new forms of value.

In this chapter, we will use the case of Hotel Co working with RoadWarriors, a global professional services organization. Hotel Co is a global US-based company.[1] The company has several hundred hotels around the world, typically located in large urban areas and catering to a mostly upscale clientele.

RoadWarriors is one of the largest professional services companies in the world.[2] Because RoadWarriors's staff frequently travels to their clients' sites in major US cities, RoadWarriors is identified as a strategic account by Hotel Co and the firm dedicates a full-time strategic account manager to the account. Although RoadWarriors is a global firm, regulatory requirements prevent the firm from being managed globally, so we will only consider the US component of their business in this chapter.

---

[1] Hotel Co is a fictitious name to protect the confidentiality of the real company.
[2] RoadWarriors is a fictitious name to protect the confidentiality of the company.

1 Adapt Your Problem Formulation to What the Other Party Wants to See Addressed

In step 1 of the relationship-building, you, as a SAM or senior buyer, will have hypothesized a problem formulation. In step 2, you will discover what your *alter ego* has in mind. Be prepared for significant give-and-take and, in some cases, outright renunciation of the original problem statement and replacement by something completely different. Listen attentively. If anything, be prepared to err on the side of overstating how far you are willing to move from your original formulation; your partner will give you a lot of credit for flexibility. Some of the best co-creation efforts have been borne from spectacular mis-formulations of the original problem. Do not hesitate to publicly abandon your original intent and create a new one if this is what the situation demands. And of course, if your problem formulation turns out to have legs, then run with it.

In early 2014, the Chief Purchasing Officer of RoadWarriors, Bob Chase, realized that his organization spent a lot of time working on the RFPs sent to them by all of the major hotel chains.[3] He estimated the total number of hours dedicated to each major hotel chain as between 2,500–3,000 hours per year and he thought it was a highly unproductive use of his staff's time. Chase comes from the automotive industry where procurement plays a key role in overall competitiveness of the business. Working at RoadWarriors is a bit of a second career for him, and he decided to bring some of the purchasing sophistication of the automotive industry to the professional services industry, where procurement is not necessarily as "strategic". He decided he would try to find a SAM in a hotel chain that was willing to experiment with him on a new and improved procurement process they would devise together. He challenged George Fields, the head of Hotel Co's Strategic Account Management program, to come up with a better system by working with him on the new concept.

Here is what Chase observed.[4] The RFP process, before the eventual transformation it underwent, lasted close to five months, from August until late December. RoadWarriors provided Hotel Co with an estimated number of nights, by major cities, for the upcoming year and invited Hotel Co to provide bids from their list of about 500 hotel properties for those cities, then

[3] Source: multiple interviews with Bob Chase, RoadWarriors.
[4] Source: multiple interviews with George Fields, Hotel Co Hotels.

compared the Hotel Co bids to competitors. The RoadWarriors senior buyer then selected the Hotel Co properties they were interested in, and communicated his decision to Hotel Co. The two companies then engaged in a hard-nosed negotiation for each selected property.

The principal dimension of the negotiation was to reach agreement on a single price per property for the year, irrespective of whether the room was booked in low or high season. This yearly price was the object of numerous back-and-forth iterations for each hotel over a matter of months. Ultimately, the negotiation expanded to multiple other factors, such as last room availability, free Internet access, free breakfast, and club privileges, producing additional rounds of discussion. There were endless emails, faxes, phone calls, and multiple change of courses along the way.

Chase found out that Fields had largely been traveling on the same path, wondering what value was added in this endless back-and-forth of negotiation between the two firms. Hotel Co's problem was the mirror image of RoadWarriors's: Fields could visualize the large amount of wasted time on the Hotel Co side in responding to these RFPs. Every year, the Hotel Co strategic account manager orchestrated a complex and professionally unrewarding ballet of property revenue managers submitting their bids and iterating back-and-forth with RoadWarriors buying staff as the negotiation progressed on each property. He had long sought a creative senior procurement person who would be willing to experiment with dynamic rather than fixed pricing. Chase at RoadWarriors offered him this unique opportunity.

2   Create a Face-Off Plan for Each Stream of Work You Design and Recruit the Team Members Needed for the Effort on Both Sides

Once your problem is defined, work with your SAM, or senior buyer partner, to identify not only who "owns" the problem and needs to participate in the core team, but also who needs to be consulted or involved in providing the information, or the systems infrastructure, for its resolution. Don't treat this as the quick building of a list that you can rapidly discard after a first meeting. Think of every member of the problem-solving group as a person whose heart and mind you will need to win. Most efforts fail because of the SAM's, or senior buyer's, failure to sustain the interest of all parties along the way. When people stop coming to your meetings and start sending delegates, do know that you are in trouble. When you lose the "work with" partner in a department you've been working with, initiate a new charm offensive as if working from scratch. In some cases, SAM s and senior buyers even miss an entire constituency. IT is frequently "forgotten" in the design of some efforts, for which there is hell to pay later since IT platforms are an essential ingredient of co-creation.

Make your effort ostensibly small at the beginning, as you will likely have to justify why you need to mobilize so many people, how much of their time you will need, and why your project should come ahead of competing demands for the employees time, as administered by the firm's Project Management Office. Later on, you will be able to increase your demands for resources as you will have earned the right through early successes to ask for more people.

At the outset, the Hotel Co-RoadWarriors story did not involve a terribly complex community-building effort on either side; a lot happened between Fields and Chase at the senior level. There were a few meetings between Fields, accompanied by his strategic account manager, and Chase, supported by one of his senior staff members. That's all it took to agree that simplifying the complex RFP process ought to be the problem they work on together. The two men also agreed that if the two companies figured out a way to reduce their respective costs, they should be doing more business together. They now had a framework and business case for engagement.

Very quickly though, both parties realized they had to involve a larger set of players if the basic negotiation process between the two firms was to be revamped. It is one thing to say "we want to do more business together because we have redesigned our negotiation process", but another to make it happen across the huge mass of RoadWarriors traveling employees who all have specific hotel preferences, and Hotel Co property managers used to negotiate their own prices for their property.

On the RoadWarriors side, the Procurement group run by Bob Chase is accountable for the negotiation process, but they work through a large sister organization, the Operations Group, that runs the programs and systems through which consultants pick hotels in their day-to-day work. This is, of course, where the proverbial rubber hits the road. Each RoadWarriors employee makes reservations as a function of their individual preference and client context, and (reluctantly) within corporate constraints. For example, the web site they enter their reservation on steers them to particular hotels as a function of corporate agreements that have been negotiated. The ultimate decision is made by the traveling individual (or his/her assistant). There is often a lot of tension between the desires of the ferociously independent consultants of RoadWarriors and the strategic direction provided by corporate Procurement and Operations. In particular, delivering on the wish to potentially steer more business toward Hotel Co as a reward for participating in a joint streamlining of the negotiation process required enlisting the Operations Group into the effort. This became one of Chase's priorities.

Similarly, on the Hotel Co side, the RoadWarriors SAM had to make all the revenue managers in the relevant properties comfortable with the notion of a new, more centrally-driven negotiation process. Massive herding of the cats was also needed on the Hotel Co side, since revenue managers consider pricing as a jealously guarded local prerogative.

3   Get the Team Mobilized and Aligned on the Formulation of the Problem

There are many ways of running a meeting that aims to mobilize and align a team on a common goal, and most of them have been well-known since the early days of the quality, reengineering, work-out, Six Sigma or Agile Programming movements. As a general rule, live meetings work best whenever people can be economically brought together in one place. While co-creation is heavily data-driven at its core, it also relies on the human bonding of individuals coming together with a transformative purpose, which is best achieved through live contact. One proven moment of camaraderie-building involves off-hour eating, drinking and socializing in the ritual known as "team dinners". Since most organizations are global, though, practicality may dictate that the first meeting of the team be a web chat, a video- or regular phone conference.

There was no grand meeting of the Hotel Co and RoadWarriors sides, no large gathering of people since the people involved at both firms were geographically scattered across multiple US cities. Chase and his senior project manager drove the project on the RoadWarriors side, painstakingly rallying the revenue managers of some of the major hotels to the value of the new approach. Fields and his SAM did the same on the Hotel Co side.

4   Agree on the Specific Hypotheses You Want to Tackle

Solving the problem you have jointly agreed to tackle requires developing a hypothesis on how to solve it. At the first formal meeting or call involving both teams, be sure to allocate some time to idea generation on the root causes of the problem and possible ways to address these issues. The classic rules of creativity apply here, such as "there is no such thing as a bad idea", or "try to build on the idea of others rather than dismiss them". Be prepared to have subject matter experts in the room who will express doubt that any external party to their domain can make a valuable contribution.

Encourage hypotheses that involve some kind of measurable quantity. The idea behind co-creation is that there is a pattern of correlation between variables that you're trying to discover, i.e., some causes drive some effects, and if you can formulate a path on how various variables relate to each other, you can then measure these variables and see whether you were right or wrong in the first place. It will take a while for these patterns to be formulated as a full system, and even more time to put in place a measurement system that allows you to see whether you were right, but the more analytical the hypotheses developed in the first meeting, the better.

Not everybody will be able to contribute at this level of measurable specificity. You will likely receive input such as "the entire culture of our firm is to blame," which may be true, but is not directly actionable. When people make broad statements of this type, try to push participants toward giving you practical examples of the broad issue, which can then bring you closer to metrics you can observe and try to influence.

From the conversations between Chase and Fields a simple idea emerged. A lot of the negotiation complexity between the two firms arose from the fact that the value of a hotel room is highly contextual. Getting a room in New York during Fashion Week costs a lot more than getting that same room on a weekend in mid-February. Chase understood and accepted that Hotel Co valued each of its hotel rooms differently at different periods of the year, but had a tough time modeling what the acceptable price curve for RoadWarriors ought to be. A lot of the negotiation energy (and cost) on the RoadWarriors side was aimed at peaking behind the Hotel Co curtain, understanding the dynamics of hotel occupancy for each property, and trying to erode away the putative "unreasonable premium" that Hotel Co was perhaps trying to hide in its rate.

Chase put the burden of providing competitive information on Fields. He asked him to give him his best picture of the competitive situation of each particular hotel at any time. He sketched out a map with the property at the center, competing properties around, and a dashboard showing some data on occupancy and rates for the Hotel Co property and said, "If you give me this information, together we can price the rooms for RoadWarriors that optimize your revenues and minimize my costs; it will be a win-win." He made it clear that he was not trying to apply brute force to the negotiation, but intended to create a joint improvement by removing the lack of transparency that existed on the competitive situation.

Fields was pretty amazed. He had historically not seen a lot of thought leadership coming from senior buyers at major customers. Chase was introducing a novel view of thinking about pricing and negotiating. It was admittedly still a bit theoretical still, but there was something tempting to the concept. And Fields had an idea….

5   Envision the Platform and Process Through Which You Will Gather the Needed Data

As we've already seen, the best platforms are those that already exist, so with the help of your "work with" partner, take an inventory of the existing systems of both firms, with the thought (or hope?) that some of the data from these existing systems can be made transparent to the partner and will generate new opportunities at the intersection of both firms. Make sure you have IT path-finders at each firm to guide you through the maze of systems both firms have and ask them what each system does.

Chances are your IT partners will be able to think of ways to make some proprietary internal data available to your partner at fairly low cost, even if it means starting with a rustic, cobbled-up periodic batch report that guides the early joint analysis. There will be plenty of time in stages three through six of the relationship-building process to build a more permanent, elegant link and dashboard, so don't insist on sophistication early on. Old data will probably prove difficult to extract and export outside the company's boundaries because it will likely be inextricably linked with the program itself. There may also be significant regulatory or security barriers that make it difficult, or impossible, to let an outside entity come "read" internal data. The general trend in IT development is toward modularity and transparency, though, so you'll likely experience that making data transparent across firms slowly improves over time.

Some people call this approach of making internal data transparent to the partner "opening up the kitchen" or "creating a glass house". Whatever the metaphor, as a SAM, imagine what the senior buyer could do with the sales data you look at internally, if it became available to him. Would that create new insights for him? Today, you probably conduct some form of sales analysis, try to detect patterns, maybe identify price or quantity trends. Would he learn something of use for her own business from the work you already do today, but do not yet publish? As we already saw with BD, sales and sourcing data are not always the mirror of each other, given the inefficiencies of IT systems, and senior buyers can learn from suppliers' analyses of the customer's purchases.

Or alternatively, as the senior buyer, think of how the SAM might benefit from seeing this data. As a SAM, your first reaction will likely be: "Oh, but if I did, he would know the cards that I hold and would negotiate my price down." As a senior buyer, you may be thinking: "But this would take away all my leverage." Neither is necessarily true. Knowledge does not have to be a win-lose situation. It can be win-win if the two of you, SAM and senior buyer, can come up with a better answer as a result of the transparency you have created for each other.

And if all those attempts at opening up the IT kitchen fail, create a one-off, *ad hoc*, paper and pencil approach that attempts to generate new original data-based insights by crunching numbers across both firms (OK, technically, it might be an Excel spreadsheet on a PC rather than pencil and paper!). This is, after all, how analytical work supporting business-to-business sales used to be conducted, until the new resources of the cloud, analytics and other Internet of Things technologies became available! And if the brute force, one-off analysis proves sufficiently potent, try to convince someone in IT that a platform that automates what you did as a one-off would bring huge benefits. Needless to say, your chances of success in getting a platform initiative started from scratch in this fashion are not very high, but it is worth a try.

Back at Hotel Co, Fields realized he had a potentially simple answer to the challenge raised by Bob Chase at RoadWarriors. He suggested making Hotel Co's revenue management system transparent to RoadWarriors and using it as the foundation for the new pricing model with RoadWarriors. Hotel Co, like all major hotel chains, has long had in place a computer-generated revenue management system that calculates the Best Available Rate (BAR) for any property at any given time, as a function of the known and anticipated supply-and-demand situation for that property and its competitive environment. The system updates the price of each room, every day, every hour, and sometimes every minute. This system was being used internally by each hotel's revenue manager to price the available rooms for maximum revenue. All Hotel Co had to do was make the data available to RoadWarriors and set the RoadWarriors's price off that BAR price. From an IT standpoint, this was a fairly simple project that could be implemented within a few weeks.

RoadWarriors of course still wanted to leverage its purchasing clout with Hotel Co. The two firms agreed on a single percentage discount that RoadWarriors would receive "off BAR" for any night at any hotel anywhere. Just one number for the year! This discount percentage number was to be the object of intense negotiation, but arriving at one number proved a lot easier than negotiating individual rates for a large number of hotels over 365 days a year. The goal was to create a drastic cost reduction. The other advantage of the new concept was that hotels would no longer have to sacrifice valuable rooms with lower-priced RoadWarriors people showing up at peak times, and RoadWarriors would no longer have travelers reporting back to headquarters that other people at the hotel were getting more favorable rates during non-peak periods.

6   Experiment with the New Platform and See What the Data Shows

Now you have a platform in place, most commonly, a crude solution that is good enough for now, and you start gathering data. Two things are likely to happen. First, your data is likely to not be very clean at the outset, sometimes to the point of being meaningless. Do not get discouraged by the early noise. Just scrub, scrub and scrub until you find a little corner of the data that allows you to create meaning, and market the hell out of that timid insight you have created. Second, the data may not go into the direction you had anticipated. Some correlations you had hypothesized may be non-existent. At Hotel Co and RoadWarriors, the system came alive in early 2014 and the two companies started tracking outcomes in the first four months of the year. They agreed to track total RoadWarriors' revenues at Hotel Co, number of room nights, and average price per room. They also tracked what result the new system was producing vs. what it would have produced in the traditional negotiation process. Although they did not have the means of tracking cost on either side, they both agreed to rely on a "gut feeling" to see whether they were indeed successfully eliminating some redundant negotiation work.

The early results proved encouraging. RoadWarriors' revenues at Hotel Co were up significantly. The price per room was lower, on average, for RoadWarriors, even after accounting for mix issues, but as RoadWarriors was redirecting competitive volume to Hotel Co, Hotel Co volume was up overall. Most importantly, RoadWarriors' people were deploying themselves more effectively to Hotel Co hotels as a function of where they were most needed by Hotel Co, instead of flocking to inadvertently underpriced hotels, or generating bad feedback, because they were overpaying for largely unused hotels. Most importantly, the relationship felt win-win, and everybody looked forward to a dramatically simplified, less costly negotiation process a few months later.

7 Design and Scale the New Process of Interaction Based on the New Platform You Have Devised

You're now on solid ground because you have created a flow of data between your respective firms and either confirmed or rejected your original hypothesis. If the data proves you wrong, go back and formulate a better hypothesis and try again (or else go back to beating up on each other and forget cocreation!). If the data goes in the general direction you had intended, you're in business. Your next job is to start thinking of how the two firms will hardwire their new mode of interaction, based on the new platform and data they have installed. The collective supplier-customer system is now smarter than it was before, but much work remains to be done to translate the insights provided by the platform and the data into an actual design of the decision-making processes and policies through which the two firms will work in day-to-day interactions.

The first process to be redesigned between Hotel Co and RoadWarriors was the price negotiation process itself and its corollary, the risk management process associated with that price. On one end, the two firms had agreed that there would be only one element to be negotiated—the percentage discount granted by Hotel Co to RoadWarriors off the Best Available Room price (or BAR)—which made for a comparatively easy process (albeit with high stakes).

There was great trepidation on both sides, however, on the issue of whether the new system was going to produce a winner and a loser. The experiment period had been encouraging in that regard, but both firms were still largely venturing into the unknown, fearing that the new system might suddenly produce unintended consequences and allow one of the two companies to gain at the expense of the other. To prevent this, the two firms agreed at the outset that the purpose of the new system was not to outsmart each other and have one of the party gain at the expense of the other. As a result, both firms were comparing the actual prices yielded by the new system with what the old prices would have yielded, and agreed to adjust the discount percentage if it proved detrimental to one of the two firms. In other words, the goal of the system was not to produce a winner and a loser as in the traditional sales and procurement system, but to eliminate unnecessary RFP costs on both sides, thereby guaranteeing a double win. Imagine that; a procurement manager working collaboratively with a sales department to jointly eliminate a "reciprocally inflicted" cost, and agreeing *a priori* to share the spoils rather than fight over them! Ultimately, there have been even greater rewards for both firms.

Beyond the high-level price and risk management processes we just discussed, the two firms also had to redesign all the micro-negotiation processes linking individual Hotel Co hotels to RoadWarriors in order to accommodate the new more centrally-driven system. As one can imagine, this took a bit of effort, particularly in a highly decentralized environment where Hotel Co does not own, or manage, all of its hotels. Allowing a central pricing system to "take over" required a lot of work on the part of Hotel Co to convince individual managers to let go of their pricing prerogative.

8   Unleash a Current of Personal Empathy Between Key Players

Ultimately, the rational and analytical constructs of co-creation that we have discussed so far as part of our stage two in the relationship-building process can only take the sales-procurement relationship so far. Early on in stage two, an emotional energy flow needs to start developing across members of both firms, enabled by the infrastructure you have put in place. If people do not like each other, no matter how sophisticated the platform, the co-creation will not take effect.

In phase two of the business-to-business relationship development process, you need three transformational forces to be liberated. First, the vision of the transformed relationship must be viewed as compelling by the staff on both sides, which requires massive communication to all interested parties (the old adage remains true that one cannot over-communicate). Second, individuals need to be able to visualize a dramatically improved view of their personal future work experience, and the best way for employees to visualize their "to be" experience is to personally work on its design. Thirdly, employees need to feel that the person on the other side of the supplier-customer divide is a person they want to see win. This third part—the flow of empathy that links employees across companies—is what ultimately provides the energy flow of transformation. Contrary to the popular saying that familiarity breeds content, familiarity, in the corporate world, breeds empathy. And familiarity comes from working with each other long enough to experience success together.

Like with all firms, the cultures of Hotel Co Hotels and RoadWarriors are a mix of analytical and rational elements on one end, and emotional aspects, on the other. While the transformation of the negotiation process across both firms may not appear to be terribly emotional, it is symptomatic that both leaders of the transformation have invested themselves deeply into this effort and created a personal legacy through it. For George Fields at Hotel Co, the relationship with RoadWarriors has proven to be a creative breakthrough in the design of his new strategic account management organization and has paved the way for the development of a new, more innovative mode of corporate sales relationship within Hotel Co. For Bob Chase, the effort has proven that procurement can be strategic in a professional service firms and that thought leadership can be found not only within the divisions of the firm, but also in its shared services organization.

9   Identify Early Value Created and Create a Buzz Around It

The main role of the data platform put in place in stage two is to start capturing results. The accumulation of early data allows for building a war room around the data platform, which in turn allows the team to communicate early successes. Thirty or forty years ago, reengineering consultants learned the value of having a physical place where participants in a change initiative can congregate and share stories of early accomplishments. The modern version of the war room, like its military equivalent, is data-enabled and utilizes the *son et lumière* quality of the latest digital visualization technologies, but it proceeds from the same logic of featuring quasi-live data and generating a social and emotional dialogue around it.

As soon as you have data, no matter how fledgling or unproven, start publicizing it. Because of the analytical tradition of many businesses, managers or employees often want to wait until they have boardroom-level reliability before sharing their data. Don't! Put the data out, with all necessary caveats, and create a buzz around it. Invite people to start playing with it. Do this, not only to showcase the data in its raw analytical form on a small PC screen, but project it in flashy giant chart forms on the walls of the war room. Analytical data is valuable, but "data in your face" triggers the emotions that precipitate action. Your role as a SAM, or senior buyer is to trigger intrigue, or even guilt, or at the minimum, curiosity. Be a data *provocateur*. If your data is wrong or incomplete, people will show you why and help you correct it. They will identify resources in both firms that can help make it better. The data set will expand from what you have created, because your colleagues will want to add their stone to your edifice. Unexpected individuals will come forward and suggest new algorithms you may want to investigate, allowing co-creation not only of the data itself, but also of the algorithms that will allow your respective firms to make sense out of that data.

Today, the co-creation program linking Hotel Co Hotels and RoadWarriors has created significant value on both sides. Hotel Co sales at RoadWarriors are significantly up and continue to grow faster than the market average. RoadWarriors customer satisfaction with Hotel Co is also significantly up. Transaction costs between both firms have come down significantly as a result of the disappearance of the RFP process.

Figure 5.1 summarizes how George Fields at Hotel Co and Bob Chase at RoadWarriors constructed the transformational agenda for their relationship.

10   Envision How the Initial Platform Can Be Expanded to Create New Forms of Value

In stage two of the relationship-building process, your role is to put in place a crude platform that can expand in multiple directions, and to build trust and empathy through a core team that will drive both parties to want to do more with each other. When both are in place, there's no telling how far the scope of the co-creation will expand.

Neither Hotel Co, nor RoadWarriors are yet in a position where the data they have accumulated through the dynamic pricing platform can yet be mined at the property level, but this may well be the next step. The foundation the two firms have created opens the door for more value creation opportunities,

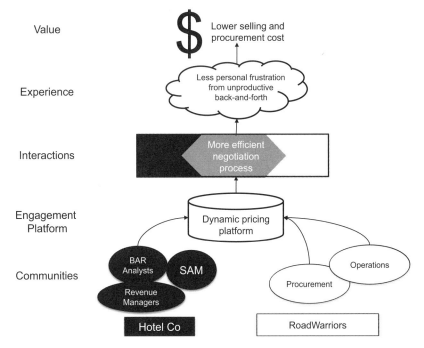

Fig. 5.1 Co-Creation Value Map for Hotel Co and its Roadwarriors professional services firm customer. This chart is also available at http://www.eccpartnership.com/the-co-creation-edge.html

for example by creating teams of local property managers at Hotel Co working with frequent RoadWarriors travelers at that location, jointly devising promotion, or special service programs, uniquely suited to these local properties. Hotel Co is also considering dedicating specific resources to RoadWarriors travelers in some hotels, such as offering a dedicated check-in desk, or concierge services to RoadWarriors travelers.

In this chapter, we reviewed what happens in the second stage of the relationship-building process, as supplier and customer engage in an early dance with each other. We highlighted the work they need to do to envision the value they can create together, and how they can assemble a joint team to pursue that value. The next step is to Engage as a Team and Connect Emotionally, which is covered in the next chapter.

CHAPTER 6

The Date: Engage as One Team and Connect Emotionally

Y ou have now held your first workshop together and agreed on a forum where both supplier and customer will meet to determine if there is value to be created together. Both parties have agreed to commit investigative resources to the development of a joint project, and there is some expectation that a long-term relationship may develop at the end of this stage. Both supplier and customer have lined up a team, and they now have to figure out how to engage with each other.

In our human relationship metaphor, it is time to go on a date together. You're not yet sure what the other party wants to do, but you've both been on dates before and know enough to suggest possible venues. It takes a lot of discussion to figure out what the evening is going to be like, how to organize it, who will pay for what, and where this should go after that. At some point, though, you just have to engage and see what happens. You have qualified the other party enough to know there is some attraction, but both also know how fleeting those first impressions can be. You are past romantic dreaming about your partner and you've danced together, but you're not yet sure yet where all this will lead.

Once again, the ten phases of the co-creation cycle have transformed into something else now that we are in the third step of the relationship-building cycle:

1. Deconstruct the problem into its components and organize into streams of work.

2. Progressively discover whom to engage on each stream of work.

3. Ensure that each team develops a structured process of engagement, has the necessary tools and creates a regular review schedule.

4. Help each team develop an explicit articulation of a hypothesis on how it will solve each problem.

5. Figure out what data platform you can use, or build, to generate data and introduce that platform.

6. Crank the data and invite interpretation of its meaning.

7. Create frequent give-and-take updates, over-communicate, tell stories and over-react to guidance.

8. Create excitement toward change.

9. Aggregate early value, estimate ROI and price-qualify your partner.

10. Create a delivery project plan.

In this chapter, we will use the case of Pellets (name changed), a large chemical company manufacturing engineered polymer resins,[1] working with Autoparts (name also changed), a supplier to the automotive industry that makes molded parts for cars.[2] Autoparts is known as a "tier 1" supplier. The car industry uses a hierarchy of vendors who make specific parts for the car (electronics, chassis, body, seats, etc.) and, in an effort to streamline the number of suppliers large car manufacturers have to deal with, many years ago, they structured vendors and suppliers into a tier system. The companies that supply the automotive manufacturers directly are known as Tier 1 suppliers. There are few Tier 1 suppliers globally, and they tend to be multi-billion dollar companies.[3] Autoparts is one of them. These Tier 1 suppliers are the customers of Tier 2 suppliers who make smaller parts fitting into the parts assemblies that become part of the finished product. Historically, Autoparts used to be a division of a major car manufacturer and was spun off a few years

---

[1] For a brief introduction to engineering polymers (also called engineering plastics), see Wikipedia entry on engineering plastic at https://en.wikipedia.org/wiki/Engineering_plastic.

[2] For an understanding of the role of engineered polymers in the car industry, see the September 2014 report from the American Chemistry Council's Economic and Statistics Department, available at http://www.plastics-car.com/lightvehiclereport.

[3] For a list of the largest automotive suppliers and their sales, see Statista report available at http://www.statista.com/statistics/199703/10-leading-global-automotive-original-equipment-suppliers/.

ago into an independent publicly listed company. It now caters to all major automotive manufacturers in the US, Europe, Japan and Latin America.

Pellets is a large global manufacturer of diversified chemical products, and the engineered polymers division, the case studied in this chapter, is one of the largest divisions of the group, with manufacturing plants located around the world.

The challenge for Pellets' SAM was to avoid the commodity trap i.e., act merely as a product supplier without providing any other technical value-added services. Although supplier-customer relationships have improved quite a bit in the last few years, particularly since the re-birth of the US automotive industry after its collapse in the early 21st century,[4] the temptation remains strong on the part of automotive buyers to exert their power and intimidate suppliers into a price-only game.

As it happens, the senior buyer for resins at Autoparts was a bit of a maverick in his organization. Like his colleagues, he knew he had to drive the cost of resins down to a reasonable price. But because he was a technical person himself, he also knew that engineered resins are tricky to handle, because they are placed in a mold and "cooked" to demanding specifications. This requires the automotive supplier's R&D department to design both the part and the mold, two costly and delicate operations that demand a lot of knowledge from the automotive supplier about the interaction between the resin, the mold and the part. Once the part is designed and in production, a whole new challenge awaits: one of productivity and cost, given the high volume of parts that need to be manufactured for every car model and the competitive cost pressures of the industry. At the production stage, Autoparts has to place the resin in the mold, bring it to very high temperature, get the formed part out of the model, verify its quality, and finally send it to parts sub-assembly and final assembly—and do all of that very fast and at low cost.

Recently, the Pellets' SAM, during one of his routine calls on one of the Autoparts manufacturing plants in Ohio, was told by the Autoparts plant manager that the resins senior buyer at corporate headquarters had been an engineer at the plant before joining the procurement group. Together, plant manager and SAM decided to call him and see whether he'd be interested in

---

[4] For a description of how the US automotive manufacturers have fared in recent history against international competitors, see the July 2015 report from the American Auto Council http://americanautocouncil.org/sites/default/files/2015-AAPC-Economic-Contribution-Report(FINAL).pdf.

sponsoring a new initiative where Pellets would seek to create new sources of value for Autoparts, using the Ohio plant as pilot. The senior buyer agreed to launch an exploratory phase, of a few weeks, which they called Analysis & Design. The co-creation effort had started.

1   Decompose the Problem into Its Components and Organize into Streams of Work

As a SAM, you have now been given license to hunt in the customer's operations, thanks to the preparatory work you did in step one of the relationship-building process and the limited engagement you've had with some of the supplier's staff in step two. You can now bring in the expertise of some of your firm's colleagues and deploy them in the customers' organization. Facing you, the senior buyer has agreed to the approach, accepting that the relationship will not be solely driven by price and terms, and allowing involvement of technical people in the supplier's organization. The senior buyer is mobilizing the right operational people on the supplier's side and partnering with the SAM in designing how they should work together.

Before creating the face-off plan, however, SAM and senior buyer must agree on the opportunities they want to pursue together and the analyses they want to perform. By now, they should have (from the previous two phases) a general description of the problem they are trying to solve, but this problem needs to be broken down into sub-problems that relevant knowledgeable resources can be marshalled against. This can be done using formal processes of cause-and-effect mapping (one of the best known one involves building so-called Ishikawa charts[5]), or it can be done informally by carving out the problem into various components that functional specialists are assigned to.

At Pellets, the SAM and senior buyer knew shop floor productivity was the most important issue (they internally referred to it as the "red issue"). The Ohio plant's immediate need was to deliver against quality, delivery and profit commitments made to corporate. The ability to respect the production schedule and deliver the manufactured part within a tight window was particularly key, given the just-in-time production model followed by the

[5] For a definition of Ishikawa chart, see Wikipedia entry at https://en.wikipedia.org/wiki/Ishikawa_diagram.

automotive industry and its suppliers.[6] The Ohio plant carried a very small finished parts inventory (two days or less), and any quality problems caused by the engineered polymer affected the customer's supply chain within a matter of days, creating delivery disruptions on a massive scale. Compounding the problem, engineered polymers' purchases accounted for only 3% of the plant's $400 MM revenue, but as the plant manager put it, "we don't want to see 3% of our revenue be the cause of 50% of our manufacturing problems."

The Autoparts plant manager dreamed of a robust material that would offer such low viscosity variation that it would be "idiot-proof". He argued that a competitor had a better, more forgiving resin that did not result into production interruptions. He described the shop floor problems as warpage and brittleness of the part causing processing problems downstream: stuck parts in the mold and the cavity freezing off in the winter.

The Pellets SAM pointed out there was only so much one could "bake" into the resin. He suggested breaking the problem into sub-problems and organizing them into streams of work that could be pursued more or less independently.

Figure 6.1 describes how the SAM mapped out the overall approach at Autoparts.

The SAM suggested first separating the production from the design issues. "Let's first see how we can reduce the quality breakdowns on the production line," he suggested. He thought this might have something to do with operator training. The plant manager conceded that the presence of an engineering staff during the day shifts mitigated a lot of the problems, and many of the problems came during the night shift when operators were left mostly on their own. This became the first stream of investigation.

The SAM suggested a second avenue of joint exploration: "Better control of the manufacturing protocols on the molding machines themselves might also play a role". The SAM also suggested: "An analysis of production data might suggest setting up Autoparts' production parameters differently". This became the second stream of work.

And then there was the design issue. Detroit R&D loved to design complex parts, which required the development of hard-to-make molds by the

[6]Toyota is generally credited with having pioneered the Just-in-Time production system. An introduction to the concept is provided on their web site at http://www.toyota-global.com/company/vision_philosophy/toyota_production_system/just-in-time.html.

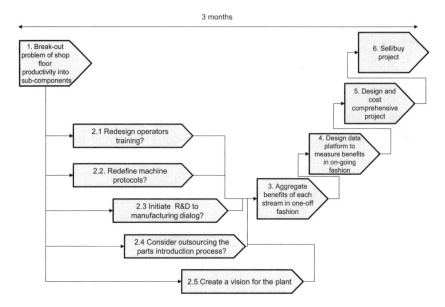

Fig. 6.1 How Pellets structured its Analysis and Design effort at Autoparts. This chart is also available at http://www.eccpartnership.com/the-co-creation-edge.html

tool designers. There was minimal dialogue between central R&D and the plant, which resulted into parts that were hard to make on an industrial scale. This became stream three.

Finally, the process of introducing the new part and mold into the manufacturing plant, even if properly designed from a content standpoint, was disruptive of the high-volume production process in the plant, because the many back-and-forth iterations between design and production tied up valuable production capacity. This became work stream four.

And this was just the beginning. As the Analysis and Design phase progressed, the Pellets team discovered the Autoparts plant faced many other issues.

2   Discover over Time Whom to Engage on Each Stream of Work

As a SAM or senior buyer, you now have a breakdown of the larger problem into its components. Your next task is to figure out who needs to be engaged on both sides in the various streams of work that will tackle those sub-problems. Start with the organizational chart and identify the functional specialists that "own" the area that is most central to the work stream: the quality department for a quality problem, the shop floor operating people for a manufacturing problem, etc. Try to recruit those people for your work stream, because they will have to drive the implementation of your design, but do not limit yourself to them. The most effective teams are multidisciplinary, so add people outside the functional area that will bring a different perspective. This can be individuals who are at the next stage in the value chain, for example, application engineers who have to deal with the consequences of a manufacturability problem caused by a production defect, or even sales people who sell the products. These people can be upstream of the area being analyzed, such as the technical people for a raw material, or an equipment manufacturer used in the production process. Generally, you will want to err on the side of inclusion.

Chances are you will not be able to identify all the right people the first time around. As you interview the various parties and start working with them, one of your first questions should be, "Who else needs to be involved in this?" You will not know at the outset who the right people are, but they will, so rely on them to give you names, email addresses and phone numbers. Ask the people you interview for some introductions and be sure to follow up. In general, the more people are engaged, the better, even though it will take more of your time as a SAM or senior buyer. The probability of success in the development of a successful relationship between supplier and customer is largely proportional to the number of people you involve in the process.

For the Pellets SAM, the fact that the senior buyer in Detroit had been an engineer at the Ohio plant proved to be a godsend, because he knew both the plant and the headquarters organization. It also did not hurt that he could use the *imprimatur* of headquarters to overcome some of the initial pushback on making the right resources available. Together with the Autoparts plant manager, the three of them created a first composition of the work teams during a one-hour meeting at the plant.

For the operator training work stream one, they selected one of the best operators the Ohio plant had (to set a high standard of performance and act as a teacher) and one of the youngest, a night shift operator with an open mind and a desire to learn (to see how much improvement could result from the effort and act as a student). They surrounded them with one of Pellets' most pedagogically apt application engineers. For the production parameters work stream two, they picked one of the manufacturing engineers and a quality person at Autoparts, and Pellets contributed one R&D person from headquarters. They also invited the German manufacturer of the molding machines to provide a resource to the group. The first response of the machine manufacturing firm was to suggest that the salesman join the group, but the senior buyer at Autoparts told the company in no uncertain terms that they did not want a salesman, but a technical person, a request which was finally honored after some negotiation.

For the design of the next generation part in work stream three, Pellets contributed two R&D resources from the materials research group and Autoparts offered one engineer and one quality person. And for work stream four, dealing with the process of pre-testing and introducing new parts in the plant, they picked the business development manager at Pellets and the plant area superintendent at Autoparts responsible for the area of the plant, which was reserved for small runs and custom applications.

The SAM and senior buyer also set up a project steering committee they put themselves on, together with one senior executive from R&D on the Pellets side, and a senior manufacturing person on the Autoparts side. The SAM and senior buyer created a first draft charter for each work team and invited them to have a first meeting where they would build on the first draft they had created.

Figure 6.2 shows how the SAM at Pellets worked with the senior buyer at Autoparts to structure the co-creation project between the two firms. The

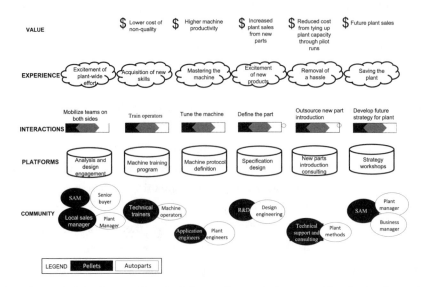

Fig. 6.2 Value Co-Creation Map for Pellets working with Autoparts. This chart is also available at http://www.eccpartnership.com/the-co-creation-edge.html

first version of the Value Co-Creation Map was less complete than what is presented here, and the rest of this chapter describes how it evolved over time as the Analysis and Design effort progressed.

They now had a structure. It was now up to the work teams to create some magic.

3   Ensure That Each Team Develops a Structured Process of Engagement, Has the Necessary Tools, and Creates a Regular Review Schedule

Now that the work teams are set up, the role of the SAM and the senior buyer is to make sure they do good work. The typical SAM and senior buyer do not usually participate in the work of each team but they can coach, cajole and monitor their progress. Sitting on project steering committees is an effective way to supervise the work, but sending email input, or offering a commentary on the project shared space, can also be quite effective, as is participating in weekly conference calls. As is logical, given their role, SAMs and senior buyers typically prioritize their participation in the work of the teams as a function of the potential size of the project during this third phase of the relationship-building cycle.

The next task is to develop a work plan with identified deliverables and a timeline. Setting a fixed deadline for completion of the work is important to keep everybody focused on the fact that the goal of the process is to arrive at a sale and a procurement contract, not conduct an exquisite analysis that goes on forever. Because the ability to develop a work plan is not necessarily a skill possessed by members of the various work teams, SAMs and senior buyer sometimes develop short tutorials on how to do that.

Some SAMs and senior buyers also teach basic interviewing skills, such as: how to develop an interview guide, how to make a friend during an interview, how to take notes and create a report, and how to follow up. They may also provide coaching notes on: how to map out processes using reengineering or quality techniques, such as Lean or Six Sigma; how to identify flow disconnects and improvement opportunities; and how to quantify the value of those opportunities and build a business case for change.

To complete some of the analytical work involved, Pellets proposed to Autoparts that they bring in an operational consulting firm to support the work of the teams on the project. Autoparts agreed to the idea, as long as Pellets paid for the consulting fees involved. As the senior buyer pointed out, "you're the one with the big upside since you stand to make a big sale, so you should pay for it". The consultants brought in the project management and consulting expertise required to support the four work streams. Their role was to maintain the pace of the project, prepare all the key meetings and do the follow-up, and provide some content expertise on measuring the cost on non-quality and business case development. They ran numerous sessions at both Pellets and Autoparts on how to design and conduct interviews, how to charter and run work teams, and how to create momentum for a large project.

They were off to the races…

4   Help Each Team Develop an Explicit Articulation of a Hypothesis on How It Will Solve Each Problem

Teamwork has both an analytical and an emotional component. The emotional side is driven by the personality of each team member and the interactions they have with each other. The analytical side comes from the ability to articulate a logical and measurable path from the problem formulation to its eventual solution, allowing for quantification of the value of solving that problem. The development of such a hypothesis is at the heart of this third phase of the relationship-building cycle. Articulating a hypothesis is a left-brained exercise that requires a mix of experience and imagination on the part of team members. They have to figure out how complex variables interact with each other based on the experience of people intimately familiar with the processes involved (insiders), aided or challenged by others who bring a fresh view of the problem (outsiders).

Because suppliers deal with similar problems with different customers, SAMs often rely on the expertise of their team to bring repeatable analytical techniques to the problems they face. Although there is great value in being able to import a fairly standard approach to a known problem, they should refrain from taking too packaged an approach, first, because it is easy to miss out on a broader solution by using a "when you're a hammer, everything looks like a nail" approach and second, because even if the answer is appropriate to the problem, customers like the idea that their solution is unique and warrants a customized approach.

The Autoparts senior buyer played a particularly helpful role in the work of stream 3, the one dealing with the introduction of new parts using engineered polymers at the Ohio plant. His hypothesis was that once the specifications of the new product, and parts, were agreed upon (this was the object of work stream 4), Autoparts should outsource the pretesting and pilot run development to Pellets, instead of keeping it in-house at Autoparts. In his mind, this would solve the problems caused by the constant back-and-forth between the R&D group of Pellets, and the procurement, engineering and manufacturing groups of Autoparts, with all the economic disruption caused to the plant by constant interruptions of schedule to accommodate the pilot runs of the new part. This was a bold proposal, first because it required Autoparts to relinquish control over a step it had historically always wanted to control, but also for Pellets, who had never formally provided this type of consulting service before.

This hypothesis and proposal represented a major challenge for the Pellets SAM, who now had to sell his management on the concept of Pellets entering the process consulting business and slowly wading into the parts manufacturing business, even though this was to be limited to small-scale pilot production. As one of Pellets' most innovative SAMs, though, he was not one to shy away from such a challenge and proceeded to sell his boss, then other senior executives outside the sales function on the concept. They gave him what they called "permission to explore".

Both SAM and senior buyer were now on unchartered territory together.

5   Figure Out What Data Platform You Can Use or Build to Generate Data and Introduce that Platform

Now that SAM and senior buyer have a hypothesis on how to solve each sub-problem, their job is to encourage various team members in the work streams to find the relevant data wherever it may be, and collect that data on a one-off basis. This data is typically not the stuff of easy computer downloads, and may be hiding in the dark corners of engineering analyses, manually kept production schedules, or critical order profitability studies conducted by the financial staff at headquarters. The job of the work team members is to scurry across multiple departments of the supplier and the customer organization, connect together previously disjointed data, and make sense of it.

SAM and senior buyers have to think at two levels during this phase. On one end, they are focused on getting one-off data that will help the sale and procurement contract to take place, so they have to pay close attention to the data and see whether it can supplement the business case and justify the project. They also have to worry about the platform side of that data, i.e., beyond the one-off sale, how will the two companies continuously refresh that data after the sale and procurement contract have been finalized? This typically requires a significant investment and the data platform is increasingly bundled as part of the sale and procurement contract. In many cases, the data platform is built into the product itself. For example, a lot of industrial process equipment, or discrete machines, come with electronic monitoring of various production, quality and engineering parameters. The same is true for medical equipment, office equipment, or the transportation industries (airplanes, trucks, car fleets). As a result, the SAM is not only selling a product, but both a product and a data platform, sometimes even a service contract built on the ability to make sense out of the data that is being generated.

Neither Pellets nor Autoparts had any preexisting data platform for any of the four streams of work they had designed. The teams, therefore, had to develop a new one. To measure the progress on the operator training work stream number one, and for the production parameters stream number two, they put in place a cost-of-quality measurement dashboard. It was a simple Excel spreadsheet recording each quality incident as it occurred, that then attempted to measure the cost of that incident in terms of hours of production lost, while categorizing the root cause of the problem in categories, such as materials defect, mold problem, operator skill, environmental issue (e.g., cold temperature), or machine problem. Agreeing on this basic qualification required hours of collaboration between the staff of Pellets and Autoparts. While the process proved tedious and generated much frustration, particularly on the Pellets side which had used this cost-of-quality nomenclature with other customers, and thought the teams should just "get on with it" instead of trying to reinvent the wheel, the Socratic discovery of what drives performance in a molding plant proved to be highly valuable in mobilizing the entire plant personnel on the issue.

The Pellets SAM negotiated with the senior buyer of Autoparts that as part of the eventual contract they would sign together, Pellets (with the help of its consulting firm) would continue running the cost-of-quality dashboard and periodically report out on progress made in shop floor productivity. By then, the two original streams of operator training and machine protocol specifications had been integrated into the more holistic cost-of-quality approach, which also included new considerations, such as optimization of the schedule to minimize molds change time, and increasing the amount of pellet recycling.

About two years later, the framework created by the two partners also became the foundation of the process control software developed jointly by the German molding machine manufacturer and Pellets, as part of the next generation of machine they developed over the ensuing two years. The Ohio plant became the beta prototype for this new software, where the machine now automatically captures all the parameters the teams originally developed and tracked by hand (and many more parameters).

A data platform was born.

6   Crank the Data and Invite Interpretation of Its Meaning

Now that you have a platform, you can begin using the data it provides. Unless you are fortunate to lift significant data off an existing platform, the chances are that your early data will be a bit crude, but this does not matter. What matters is that you use the data to illustrate the points you want to make; being anecdotal is sufficient at this stage, as long as there is a path laid out to the generation of more solid data down the road.

Be prepared for the fact that insights will usually not reveal themselves in blinding flashes. Use the hypothesis you have created to structure the data collection effort, but accept the inevitable fact that early data may not reveal a lot more than what is already known. It is OK to start with fairly trivial data and let people build on what you have. Share that data anyway, and engage the people you work with on the interpretation of that data. They may see things you do not see yourself, or, more importantly, they may formulate other data you should collect and correlate to what you have already assembled. Having everyone participate in the game of hypothesis development and data collection is one of the most powerful ways of producing insights. At a minimum, you generate a lot of goodwill for opening up the data game to others. In many cases, you will find that opening up the data expert role to stakeholders other than yourself will generate helpful ideas.

At Autoparts, the work stream pertaining to the new parts introduction process at the Ohio plant yielded the most surprising insights. Nobody had ever tracked the number of iterations a new part goes through after the R&D people had agreed to the specifications of the polymer to be used, the mold to be built and the molding machine to utilize. Much to their surprise, the team discovered there had been more than 40 back-and-forth iterations for the last two parts that had been introduced, to work out kinks in the actual production process.

The first runs in the Ohio plant showed that the color of the part was not right and the master batch additive used needed to be modified, requiring a return to Pellets R&D, and a re-work with a third-party supplier. Later on, parts coming out toward the end of the run no longer met the shock absorption properties required. Once this problem was fixed, the parts began to stick in the mold and operators wasted a lot of time trying to get them out. Each instance of this required time from Pellets R&D, application engineering and sales, which the Pellets team member quantified and evaluated at about $300,000. On the Autoparts side, the losses were even more considerable, because every run tied up a production machine that could have been used to generate sales. The Autoparts team estimated there was close to $1 million in losses created by the introduction of each new part.

This gave the Autoparts senior buyer a lot of fodder for his idea to have Pellets take accountability for managing the whole product introduction process and stop clogging the production apparatus of the plant. It was not yet clear what form this outsourcing of the new part introduction process would take, but they now had some economic parameters to play with. Anything that reduced this staggeringly high cost of $1.3 million per part would help.

7   Create Frequent Give-and-Take Updates, Over-Communicate, Tell Stories and Over-React to Guidance

Data in itself is useless, unless it produces action. The role of the SAM and the senior buyer is to communicate the data in an emotionally engaging fashion to the people who can act upon it. This requires translating dry data into human interest stories. Great SAMs and senior buyers are born raconteurs. They can take thin data and translate it into compelling stories that convince people to want to do something about those stories. Great supplier-customer relationships often start with more anecdotal than statistically significant evidence. Business cases are important to selling and procurement, but in many cases, a highly symbolic illustration through the use of an isolated incident will do more than massive amounts of analytical evidence in triggering a sale.

The sheer volume of communication matters. Do not hesitate to over-communicate. Repeat the same story everywhere. There is a viral quality to each story; tell the story in such a fashion that any person hearing the story will want to repeat it to somebody else, in a "have you heard that one" kind of fashion. Distribute the slides that tell the story, or better yet, share it in picture or video form.

How you react to the guidance you receive is as important as the way you tell the story from the data. It is easy to fall in love with one's own story and stop listening. Think of each data story as a work in progress where the recipients of the story can enrich the story and tell it their way. What they see in the way you tell the story is more important than what you tell them. If they shape the story, they are more likely to want to do something about it. Doing what somebody else tells you to do is boring. Doing what you have discovered yourself is a lot more fun, so let them invent their own interpretation of that story. Over-react to their guidance. Do not ever say, "You're just saying what I have said in a different way". Instead, err on the side of acknowledging that this is a new insight you had not had yourself, first, because it will likely be true, and second, because your chances of driving a successful conclusion of the transaction will increase if you let people shape the story behind that transaction.

At Autoparts, a story called the "manifold from hell" became the stuff of legend. A manifold is a particularly elaborate engine part, and making it out of plastic is an engineering *tour de force*. When the parts introduction work team analyzed what it had taken to get the part to a state where it could be safely and cost-effectively manufactured, it created a hand-drawn flow chart on brown butcher paper showing it had taken close to two years, involved more than 300 people, cost close to $1.3 million in development and pre-trial cost, not to mention another $1 million, and counting, in field maintenance and support cost with dealers. The manifold-from-hell brown paper travelled from the Ohio plant of Autoparts to Pellets R&D, and ended up flying all over the world as an educational module in the engineering and manufacturing training programs of both firms.

8   Create Excitement Toward Change

For SAMs and senior buyers alike, Phase 3 of the relationship-building process should be designed as a giant *crescendo*. Their role is to orchestrate the momentum-building process, relying on their respective teams as instruments of the change that will result from the upcoming transaction. The temperature should gradually rise during this phase, with people becoming more and more excited at the thought of transforming the way they conduct business as a result of the new partnership.

As a simple black and white view of what drives individuals to want to change, some people will be more easily swayed by analytical evidence of the value of changing, while others will be driven by a more emotional or instinctive sense of the need to change. You need to appeal to both, in such a fashion that the rational types nod their head knowingly at the time when you present your business case, while other more emotional types intuitively feel this is the right thing to do. When the two of them agree with each other that they need this project, you've got it made. Nothing like having the poets and the engineers agree on the need to work for a new strategic sale or procurement contract.

To get to this massive alignment of all relevant stakeholders, the key is to match people in your organization with similarly minded people on the other side. Match analytical types with analytical types and encourage them to go at it with the data, and let emotional people sell each other on the need for transformation through the new partnership.

Toward the end of the Analysis and Design phase of work with Pellets, the excitement at the plant became palpable. Something was going on that was a lot bigger than the sum of all the work streams taking place. The plant manager and his senior staff knew something was happening that had not been there before. What had started as a simple material-related shop floor problem had evolved toward a large transformational effort about the future of the plant.

As it turns out, the plant's role in the manufacturing network of Autoparts had been questioned at Detroit headquarters for some time, and the plant's management and personnel felt they had to demonstrate that they had a unique competence compared to their internal manufacturing rivals. Making hard-to-make parts from fancy engineered polymers was one of the best ways they had of creating an original positioning for the plant, thus making Pellets a lot more strategic to the plant than a regular supplier of commodity chemicals. While being technically an outsider, the Pellets SAM, because of the unique know-how his firm brought to bear, also had better access to Autoparts' Detroit headquarters people in R&D than the Ohio plant itself, so the plant's management wanted the Pellets SAM to share this compelling story of the unique capability of the Ohio plant at headquarters. They were no longer speaking of shaving a few cents off the price of a bag of resin.

The future of the plant was at stake. It couldn't get more strategic than that.

9   Aggregate Early Value, Estimate ROI and Price-Qualify Your Partner

As the end of phase three, as the relationship-building process reaches its end, and the two firms start getting ready for the closing phase, the SAM and senior buyer should start working together on adding up the value that can be created by aggregating the benefits coming from the various work streams. The idea here is to compute an aggregated savings and revenue increase value, relate that amount to the cost of the project that the customer will pay the supplier, and compute some kind of ROI (e.g., "40% over three years") or breakeven time ("this project will pay for itself in the first year").

Technically, SAM and senior buyer may have to watch for double-counting of overlapping benefits claimed by the various streams of work. For example, both the operator training and the machine optimization stream may claim the same reduction in number of incidents, or increase in machine uptime. Avoiding this double-counting phenomenon is why the correct set-up of the team at the outset of this phase is important and why having a central steering group is helpful.

Be aware that cost reduction is instinctively more highly valued than revenue increases, or investment avoidance. Your role as a SAM, or senior buyer is to keep everybody focused on the fact that cost reduction may seem to be a "sure thing" item, but growth and future savings are also important because the future of the firm depends on it.

Once you start having a rough notion of the total value of the project, start price-qualifying the other party and see how they react. The typical price qualification conversation between a SAM and senior buyer usually involves a three-part process. First, vet together the estimate of benefits the project will generate after roll-up of the various work stream's benefits, and discuss the likelihood that those benefits will effectively materialize as planned. Second, have the SAM itemize the items she would like to include in the proposal, producing a total project price. Third, the two should discuss whether the ROI of the proposed project meets the buyer's expectations of return for such a project, i.e., is the cost of the proposed project justified by the value it aims to create?

The SAM and senior buyer should price-qualify each other as early as possible in this third phase of the relationship-building process. A common mistake of rookie SAMs and inexperienced senior buyers is to operate with wildly different assumptions of total project price for too long, which can lead to a massive over-investment of resources when it turns out the customer never intended to launch a transformational project (in some cases, the supplier may also under-invest in relationship to the buyer's expectation, but this is less frequent).

At Autoparts, the discussion of value, and the price qualification conversation, took place in the following fashion: The SAM showed the senior buyer that Pellets could contribute about $10 million in benefits over the next three years; a combination of productivity increase on the shop floor (from stream 1 and 2); reduction of inefficiencies in the introduction of new parts (from stream 3); and development of a new part in the Ohio plant for a new car model being designed (new stream added at the very end of the Analysis and Design phase).

The senior buyer discounted some of the revenue estimate by arguing that future sales were, by definition, more uncertain than shop floor cost reduction, and they agreed that the total value of the business case was probably closer to $9 million (average of $3 million a year). Pellets proposal was for a three-year contract where Autoparts would pay $1.5 million for the supply of the chosen polymer (at the estimated production volume of the plant), plus another $500,000 a year in fees for Pellet placing a materials team on-site at the Ohio plant managing the parts introduction process and developing an on-the-premises lab and pilot plant. The senior buyer was pleased that a $2 million spend per year would produce a yearly $3 million saving (50% ROI) and the project would pay for itself year after year.

It became an easy decision for the Autoparts senior committee to agree to the project, particularly given the enthusiastic leadership provided by the Autoparts senior buyer and the massive support of the plant staff for the project. The Pellets SAM referred to this as "One of the easiest $4.5 million sales I ever made". The innovation involved in having an onsite lab and materials team at a customer plant also became a new offering for Pellets and was replicated several times after that.

10   *Create a Delivery Project Plan*

By now, SAM and senior buyer have a "bigger than bread box" project scope and price estimate. More discussion still needs to take place to arrive at a final scope and price (this is the object of the next chapter), but with the knowledge that they are in the same ball park, it is time to start designing the delivery project and to identify delivery resources in their respective organizations. Some people on the sales team will be staying, but there will be a need for many new faces, and the introduction of delivery capabilities will be an important element in getting the project over the goal line.

The delivery of large projects is, by definition, complex and involves laying out the calendar in terms of delivery of the products or equipment: how the equipment will be installed (if equipment is involved); what services will be provided, and by whom; what work plan they will follow; and how the benefits will be accruing and tracked. This is, once again, best facilitated in collaborations between the supplier and the customer teams. This is often the first task assigned to new team members who join in the delivery phase, allowing a last test of compatibilities between the two partners.

At Autoparts, the delivery of engineered polymers over the ensuing three years did not raise any particular issue because this was the bread and butter of the firm (Autoparts has since renewed the original contract). The development of the parts introduction onsite lab and consulting capabilities proved a bit more difficult, as Pellets had never acted explicitly as a consulting engineer before. The firm's application engineering group had done it informally, but now that Autoparts is paying for the capability, expectations are higher and Pellets struggled a bit at the beginning to develop the necessary customer service capabilities.

In this chapter, we saw how at stage three of the relationship-building process, the momentum steadily grows as the project is being finalized. In the next chapter, we see what is involved in negotiating the final scope of the project and closing it.

CHAPTER 7

The Commitment: Finalize Value, Negotiate and Close

Ultimately, the role of the SAM is to drive revenues for the firm and the role of the senior buyer is to source competitively. In co-creation, the negotiation and transaction aspects do not go away. In this chapter, we address the fourth stage of the relationship-building process, i.e., the moment where the partners finally agree on the definition of what value is being created, and negotiate how that value will be shared in a contract between supplier and customer in some form of price, quantity, revenue, or cost agreement. Many of the traditional principles of negotiation still apply. The main difference with the classic sales and procurement arm-wrestling is that all the work done by the SAM and senior buyer in the previous three phases of the relationship-building process have now led to a rich definition of the value being negotiated, with the number of decision-making or influencing parties larger and the role of data more integral than in classic selling and buying.

In our human relationship metaphor, this phase in the relationship-building process is the equivalent of the commitment that two people make when they decide to share their life together, at least temporarily (perhaps phase four is more like moving-in together!). This happens when the two people realize they are better off joining forces than staying alone. It requires that the two parties have already experienced an emotional and rational bond, and are willing to translate the positive experience of the early relationship into the promise of a happier life together in the future. To demonstrate their commitment, they make a moral or contractual engagement to each other in the presence of family, friends, and sometimes, a civil or religious authority to make the commitment official.

The ten phases of the co-creation cycle take on the following form as the closing of the contract becomes imminent.

1. Keep broadening the scope of the problem you propose to tackle up to the last minute.
2. Ensure that everybody is at the decision table who needs to be there for the go-ahead.
3. Understand the spheres of influence among all of the players on both sides, and make sure all the parties are supportive of the transaction you want to close.
4. Articulate each hypothesis as a chain of causes and effects that everyone endorses.
5. Show that you have put in place the data platform that not only demonstrates early value, but will keep generating ongoing new value.
6. With data in hand, demonstrate that the project can ensure a good return.
7. Agree on the negotiation process and close.
8. Celebrate and start recruiting the right people for the delivery phase.
9. Put in place the value-tracking mechanism for the delivery phase of work.
10. Start working on the next opportunity on the first morning after closing.

In this chapter, we will use the case of Xerox, the large global company headquartered in Norwalk, Connecticut. Historically known for its copier and printer products, Xerox has transformed itself into a services company. The company is a global leader in process and document management, able to take over activities as diverse as claims management for insurance companies, benefits management for Human Resources departments, and parking management, or traffic optimization, for entire cities.[1] In this chapter, we will

---

[1] See web site description of Xerox services at https://www.xerox.com/en-us/services. An October 2012 article by Forbes, entitled *How Xerox Uses Analytics, Big Data and Ethnography To Help Government Solve "Big Problems"*, also provides a good description of Xerox strategy. It is available at http://www.forbes.com/sites/benkerschberg/2012/10/22/

focus on Xerox's Managed Print Services division (MPS), a $3 billion division inside Xerox's larger sales empire of $19 billion.[2]

On the procurement side, we will focus on one of Xerox's customers, a large diversified chemical company seeking to gain better control over its document cost and its associated infrastructure of printers, copiers and other IT-related investment.[3] The company is considered an innovation leader in its industry, and the Xerox SAM in our story suggested to the chemical company that they explore whether their internal document management could be transformed into a source of competitive advantage to become more than a well-run, cost-effective process. The reception to the notion that Xerox was a company that could help the company innovate was initially met with skepticism, with the CFO reasserting that cost was the main focus, but, as we shall see, the Xerox team slowly earned the right to play a role in the innovation area.

1   Keep Broadening the Scope of the Problem You Propose to Tackle to the Last Minute

By now, the first three phases of the relationship-building process have unfolded. If things have gone well, there is a state of excitement on both sides, and a feeling of inevitability about the impending sale on the supplier side and the upcoming strategic procurement contract on the customer side. More than ever, the SAM and the senior buyer are in the limelight. It is time to close the contract, and this is their job *par excellence*. The typical closing cycle involves a rapid succession of enthusiastic phone calls, or meetings, with the larger group of people involved on both sides, followed by a narrowing down of meetings involving a small negotiating group anchored by the SAM and the senior buyer.

how-xerox-uses-analytics-big-data-and-ethnography-to-help-government-solve-big-problems/.

[2] See Managed Print Services section of Xerox' web site at https://www.xerox.com/en-us/services/managed-print-services. The Gardner group also provides information on the quality of various providers of Managed Print Services in its Magic Quadrant report. See for example the October 2013 report available at http://adocs.info/Gartner_Group_Study.pdf.

[3] For a discussion of how to reduce cost in the corporate office, see for example Xerox April 2009 white paper called *The Optimum Office*: *How to achieve immediate and guaranteed cost savings via a Managed Print Service*, available at http://www.xerox.com/downloads/gbr/en/x/XGS_Optimum_Office_en.pdf.

One of the most telltale signs of a budding successful relationship is when the problem formulation broadens over time. If the problem formulation in stage four of the relationship remains the same as when you started, chances are that the SAM and the senior buyer are on their way to failure, or at most, to a minimal sale or procurement contract vs. what could have been. One of the areas where the know-how of the SAM and the senior buyer expresses itself most powerfully is in the creative framing of the problem. This requires that they challenge each other on the scope of the problem they want to tackle together. One of the greatest skills required from SAMs and senior buyers lies in expanding the scope of the joint investigation and ensuring that both parties explicitly articulate in the eventual contract that the boundaries of the project have been moved outward (to avoid the dangerous "scope creep", where the supplier produces more work without getting paid for it).

The scope of problems being tackled can be expanded all the way to closing time. Great SAMs and senior buyers are not afraid to include new components into the contract until the last minute, taking advantage of the enthusiasm that has been generated on both sides by the intense collaboration that has preceded the closing. They know that it will be a while before a new window opens up to do something as bold, and they take advantage of it. Conservative SAMs and senior buyers are content to stay with a limited scope to "make sure we get something." High-performing SAMs and senior buyers take more risk and seek to "bag the elephant".

At the chemical company, the main issue was originally framed as cost reduction. The Shared Services organization, under pressure from its CFO leader, was asked to reduce both operating and investment costs in the company, and the team identified document management as a sourcing category worthy of investigation. The Xerox's SAM had been talking to the chemical company's category buyer about an engagement process offered by its Managed Print Services division (MPS) that could help the chemical company identify the magnitude of the cost and investment reduction opportunity. This process, called "Assess and Optimize" in Xerox lingo, was pitched as the first step in a three-step process of engagement that would also eventually include a "Secure and Integrate" phase two and an "Automate and Simplify" stage three.[4] The senior buyer understood the Xerox Assess and Optimize

---

[4] For a description of the three-phase approach used by Xerox' Managed Print Services division, see Xerox web site at http://news.xerox.com/news/Xerox-takes-managed-print-

process to be first and foremost a sales process, and knew his firm was in for an outsourcing sales pitch at the end of that phase, but the proposed process scratched his boss' itch and he signed up his firm for it.

We catch up with our story at the moment where the "Assess and Optimize" phase is reaching its conclusion, as the SAM and Senior Buyer have worked together successfully up to that point, and the chemical company is getting ready to commit to a long-term engagement with Xerox MPS. Much remains to be decided in the closing moment of the investigation, though—scope, price, and service level agreements remain quite open.

Our SAM, at the projector, restates for the group the problems they set out to tackle:

- Can we help you reduce your document management operating cost: consumables, labor, and waste disposal services?
- Can we help you reduce the size of your investment in the document management equipment you have all over the world?
- Can we help you make your data safer?

He pauses, then explains that two other problem statements have been added in the course of the Assess and Optimize effort:

- Can we help you reduce your environmental footprint?
- Can we help you innovate in the document management area and go beyond being cost-effective?

These last two items, while not originally included in the scope of work to be performed as requested by the chemical company, had been added by the Xerox team in deliberate "push" fashion. Slowly, the environmental and innovation managers of the chemical company, had awakened to the value being provided to them "for free", and they had become part of the joint analysis team.

Subtly, the stakes had gone up and the size of the potential contract had increased.

---

services-beyond-print. See also short Xerox video featuring Mike Feldman, President, Large Enterprise Operations, Xerox Technology, available at http://news.xerox.com/news/Xerox-takes-managed-print-services-beyond-print.

2 *Ensure that Everybody Is at the Decision Table Who Needs to Be There for the Go-Ahead*

One of the worst things that can happen in the landing phases of a big contract is to discover there are important players with a stake in the upcoming transaction that you have either failed to identify, or that have just appeared on the stage to replace a person you have been nurturing for weeks and whom you consider key to the transaction. In both situations, the best laid plan can unravel quickly. Outright omission of a player is not common, since the breadth of co-creative conversations will usually surface the person you may have missed in the early stages. More frequent is an important change of personnel among the buying or selling team at closing time.

When this happens, rely on the two weapons that you have. First, use the joint team that you have assembled to communicate their strong commitment to move forward, such that the newly appointed executive feels he cannot stem the tide and disappoint his own team. Second, rely on the data platform that you have built and the early data you have accumulated. It is easy to say no a PowerPoint deck. It is harder to destroy the platform infrastructure that is being developed and interrupt the early flow of data that points to economic benefits now, and promises even greater ones in the future.

At our chemical company, the size of the Assess and Optimize joint team had been steadily growing over a two-month period. On the chemical company side, the effort had been led by a manager in the Shared Services organization who faced off against the Xerox MPS engagement manager. Both reported out their weekly findings to their respective bosses, the senior buyer for the document management category in the chemical company, and the Xerox SAM responsible for the account. The project had high visibility in their respective organizations.

They had organized in streams of work, bringing in subject matter experts in a variety of fields, to the point where close to 50 people were associated with the project. On the financial benefits stream, the work was led by a young Xerox analyst whose findings were constantly challenged, and eventually vetted by members of the chemical company's financial staff. On the environmental side, a Xerox expert in the Assess and Optimize team was faced off against a representative of the Chief Sustainability Officer at the chemical company, who had in turn invited many representatives from various plants around the world to validate the findings in their respective geographies. On the IT stream, the security experts at the chemical company were keeping the Chief Information Officer abreast of the latest findings and recommendations from the Xerox MPS IT team. And the innovation stream of work had representatives from the chemical company's facilities management team working with R&D people from Xerox's fabled Palo Alto Research center (PARC),[5] famous for its pioneering work in the modern personal computer industry.

In addition to the joint team, the Xerox SAM and the document management category buyer had also set up a Steering Committee full of heavy-hitters in the financial, environmental, IT, innovation and general management area. The Steering Committee was to be the decision-making body, while the joint team was charged with developing the data that would allow the Steering Committee to reach the right decisions.

The final meeting had been orchestrated in two steps. First, a half-day meeting and video-conferencing call, involving a group of about 50 people to review the findings, was to take place. Second, a core team of about 10 people were to share their insights with various process owners in the global organization and a small Steering Committee of five senior people.

Simply put, the momentum toward a contract had become so strong as to be almost unstoppable, but there were many lingering questions on the magnitude of the contract to be signed.

3   Understand the Spheres of Influence Among All Players on Both Sides and Make Sure All Parties Are Supportive of the Transaction You Want to Close

Much has been written in the selling and buying literature about the various roles played by individuals in the eventual decision to move forward with a major project, or not, and about how to orchestrate the process through which the SAM can remove objections to the sale and get to a positive decision. Yes, the customer team, as seen through the eyes of the SAM has multiple types of decision-makers: authorizers who sign checks, coaches who advise, technical people who judge the quality of the analytical work done, and influencers who can convince others when they are skeptical.[6] Conversely, there are also

---

[5] See for example Forbes March 2015 article entitled *How PARC Saved Xerox*, available at http://www.forbes.com/sites/gregsatell/2015/03/21/how-parc-saved-xerox/.

[6] For a discussion of the various roles played by managers on the procurement side, see for example g2m solutions web site blog entitled the 4 Types of Buyers in a Complex B2B

different profiles of sales people as seen through the eyes of the senior buyer, some who accept the reality of the buying process of suppliers and try to play within those boundaries, and others who challenge the existing procurement process and try to redefine the problem and its solution.[7] Procurement people can gain some negotiation advantage by identifying what levels in the sales organization are able to authorize what threshold of price or discount; who can provide inside information on strategic value of the sale to the supplier; or intelligence on who listens to whom on the supplier side.

While these characterizations are helpful, they all suffer from an important shortcoming: they are too SAM- or senior buyer-centric, making the SAM or the senior buyer into a hero charged with accomplishing the extraordinary task of taking on the entire customer, or supplier organization, by themselves, instead of acknowledging that B2B sales, or procurement, is a team rather than an individual sport. As valuable as SAMs are, they do not operate in a world of one-to-many relationships where the SAM tries to convince a complex group of decision-makers and influencers on the other side, and overcome their potential objection to the sale. The same is true of senior buyers. In reality, strategic buying or selling involves a many-to-many relationships, and the design of the pairings (or groupings) of individuals in the streams of work is more important than any intrinsic characterization of each individual's psychology or role. Simply put, there are work teams that gel so well that the negotiation becomes easy, and teams that do not come together well, forcing a difficult and risky birth for the project rather than a natural and painless one.

The orchestration of the right supplier-customer pairings is an art form, a bit like food and wine pairing. It does help that people across the aisle typically share a functional craft, sometimes accompanied by a dominant psychological profile, e.g., financial people often share strong analytical proclivities and think of themselves as "number jocks", which makes them more easily compatible with each other. IT people share both a highly specific technical

---

sale, available at http://www.g2msolutions.com.au/blog/bid/104246/The-4-Types-of-Buyers-in-a-Complex-B2B-Sale.

[7] One of the most popular approaches to selling is currently the "Challenger model", described in the book *The Challenger Sale: Taking Control of the Customer Conversation*, written by Matthew Dixon and Brent Adamson, Penguin Group, 2011, see Amazon website for a more complete description of the book at http://www.amazon.com/The-Challenger-Sale-Customer-Conversation-ebook/dp/B0052REP7K.

language and are often more introverts than extroverts (although there are, of course, exceptions to this rule). The role of the SAM and the senior buyer is to make sure these pairings result in happy combinations such that at phase four of the relationship-building process, everybody is prepared to vouch for the analytical integrity of the work done and communicates enthusiasm for moving ahead with the project. As the result of each stream of work is presented, neutral participants in the meeting should feel the numbers are endorsed by the people in charge and excited about wanting to go after the identified opportunity.

At our chemical company, two dramatic events occurred in the last two weeks of the Assess and Optimize phase of work. The leading member of the Environmental, Health and Safety team on the Steering Committee was promoted to a new role away from headquarters to new responsibilities in an Asian plant of the group, producing great anxiety among the Xerox team about whether his successor could come up to speed fast enough to support the project go-ahead.

The SAM quickly gained access to the new executive and tried to convince him to endorse the project even though he'd been in place so briefly he could barely find the bathroom around his new office. It took a lot of diplomacy to convince him to participate in a one-on-one dinner and to listen to the SAM's argument that the momentum toward a joint project was so strong he should endorse the project as an early win symbol of his new leadership. The new executive was particularly interested in the innovation part of the project, and less in the nuts-and-bolt cost reduction aspects. The SAM quickly organized a session with the Palo Alto Research Center people of Xerox where they impressed the new executive with some of their recent work, showing that one could not only manage documents cost effectively, but could actually extract content from the documents once they were digitized ("smart documents").[8] Xerox showed that one could, for example, use floor plans of some of the major plants to highlight safety routes that minimized risk in case of incidents. Another application, also usable in case of emergency, could be developed to immediately identify products made in certain parts of the plant

---

[8] See for example technical article written by two PARC scientists, Evgeniy Bart and Prateek Sarkar, entitled Information extraction by finding repeated structure, 2010, and available at https://www.parc.com/content/attachments/information-extraction-finding.pdf.

from the Material Safety Data Sheets, therefore allowing the safety crew to assess the risk of particular explosions.

The other challenge came from some negative vibes communicated shortly before the final meeting by managers in one of the French plants of the group. The French plant management group notified the Steering Committee that they would not attend the final meeting, and let it be known they did not feel terribly interested in having Xerox become their provider of document management services. The SAM and the senior buyer quickly arranged to have some local French people from Xerox, and from the chemical company's shared services headquarters staff, meet with the plant management staff to understand their concerns and work to create a specific adaptation of the project to their needs, thereby earning their support for the go-ahead.

Two major disasters had been averted.

4   Articulate Each Hypothesis as a Chain of Causes and Effects that Everyone Endorses

By the time you reach the closing stages of the project, the nature of the problems you started with should have evolved into a set of crisp hypotheses you can articulate analytically, and the ownership of which you are able to assign to individual members of both organizations. In other words, you need to have hypothesis owners who stand up in front of the Steering Committee and say, "Yes, this hypothesis is solid and what is being proposed here is an effective way of proving that it will indeed help our company's bottom line."

The more work you do on the ground, the more each hypothesis becomes a crisp articulation of what causes drives which effects. If you're trying to reduce a particular cost, you need to identify the major drivers of that cost, then show what action you propose to take that will reduce each component of cost. This often results into a complex chain of causes and effects, or "if this, then that" logic. Making this logic apparent to the whole team on the supplier and customer team is a powerful way of rallying everybody around a common mental model of how the two companies will jointly solve the problem at hand. Analytical models such as strategy maps (borrowed from strategy),[9] mind maps (available from commercial software),[10] or even simple

---

[9] See the article entitled *Strategy Maps: Converting Intangible Assets into Tangible Outcomes*, written by Robert Kaplan and David Norton, Harvard Business Review, 2004.
[10] See Wikipedia entry on mind maps at https://en.wikipedia.org/wiki/Mind_map.

"goes into" maps on a flip chart (sometimes referred to through their ono-
matopoeic equivalent "gazunta") where one describes what "goes into" what
in that chain of logic, are often useful to create this common mental model.

Back to our chemical company working with Xerox Managed Print Services
division, the team rapidly identified the main drivers of printing cost:

- We have a large number of machines that have low utilization (typically less than 5%). We should increase their utilization by consolidat-
  ing the number of machines, while making sure that our users do not
  have to travel too far, or wait too long, to get their documents printed
  or copied.
- The proliferation of brands and machines engenders a high cost in managing relationships with suppliers and servicing the machines, requiring
  multiple contracts and calling different repair people. We should reduce
  the number of brands and machines that we buy (At that stage, the SAM
  is whispering in the ear of the senior buyer that Xerox might be a good
  choice for that single brand).
- We waste a lot of paper, toner and energy, which has a negative impact
  on both cost and environmental footprint. We should train our users in
  managing consumables more effectively and have more rigorous ordering and inventory control processes in place.
- Our documents are not as well protected as they ought to be. We should
  digitize more of them, place them in a more secure IT environment and
  make them easily retrievable internally.
- We carry a large investment on our books linked to the document production infrastructure (printers, copiers, servers, and so on). We could
  outsource this whole asset base and only pay an outsourcing fee (P&L
  item), which would have a beneficial effect on our balance sheet.

Formulated in this fashion, each hypothesis had become analytically
testable, and the people doing the work at the chemical company and at
Xerox had become articulate spokespeople for the integrity of the work
that had been done. Most of them also volunteered to continue working on the project after the awarding of the big contract that was under
consideration.

The SAM and the senior buyer knew they were getting close.

5   Show You Have Put in Place the Data Platform that Not Only Shows Early Value, but Will Keep Generating Ongoing New Value

As you are approaching the project's closing stage, the platform you have put in place should play two roles: First, it should have produced some early insights that give credibility to the hypothesis the SAM and the senior buyer jointly formulated at the outset of the project, i.e., it validates that there is indeed great value in working together. Second, the platform should hold the promise that much more value will be forthcoming after the contract is signed. Obviously, the former acts as the credibility-builder for the latter. Negatively framed, if your platform has not added any value during the relationship-building stage, you will face an uphill battle to sell the project.

Platforms play both an analytical and an emotional role. Analytically, they are the backbone of the value creation computation and, therefore, play an important role in justifying the cost of the project against the benefits they identify, thereby allowing an ROI or "business case" justification for the project. Its emotional role, though, is equally important. By the time you reach stage four of the relationship-building process, both organizations should feel that removing that platform (in case the project does not go ahead) would leave a giant hole in the capability of both firms and represent a major setback, therefore creating a *de facto* point of no return for both parties.

The Xerox Managed Print Services group utilizes multiple platforms as part of its Assess and Optimize approach. At the level of each building, the core team on the ground has access to proprietary Xerox software that estimates the cost and utilization of each machine. The software identifies each machine and its supplier, lifts the utilization data directly from the machine's embedded measurement devices (% of time turned on, number of documents produced, and so on), then estimates all the costs associated with that machine using standard measures (energy, maintenance, consumables). This allows the Assess and Optimize team to compute an "all in" overall document production cost for each site they analyze. This inevitably creates a sense of urgency about reducing that cost, once a site manager understands how much money is being spent on document production, and creates the space for a Xerox pitch that they can outsource the whole process for a fee and deliver the benefits identified.

Having framed the overall value computation through the cost computation platform, the Assess and Optimize team can then introduce a secondary platform, a physical space simulator, that shows how reducing the number of machines (and surreptitiously replacing those non-Xerox machines with Xerox machines) would reduce the cost at each location. The software allows one to see how physically moving machines about, or removing some machines from the shop floor and replacing them with a more centralized layout, would help reduce costs, while visualizing how much farther employees would have to walk to get access to their documents. Through a combination of physical layout visualization and background cost computation, the software shows the trade-offs between, at the extreme, allowing each employee to have their own private copier, or printer, on their desk, and having only one single central printing-copying center in the building, with all intermediaries between those extremes. Of course, this data collection effort shows that utilization is typically abysmally low for most machines, not to mention the fact that these low-utilization machines are often more used for printing kids' soccer schedules than for true business purposes. At the chemical company, this platform was also used to reassure employees that they were not going to have to travel long distances, or wait long times before getting their documents printed in the new system. The team showed that the volume they produced today was often trivial and the added distance they would have to travel, and the waiting time, only minimally increased. It is hard to argue with data.

Xerox has also developed an environmental simulator software platform that allows the Chief Sustainable Officer of the customer firm to model the carbon footprint impact of various approaches to document production. One of the most potent levers for improvement is to encourage users to utilize the two-sided printing option of copiers and printers rather than the one-sided version that remains by far the dominant printing mode. There again, the Assess and Optimize team was able to show the environmental footprint reduction that would be generated if users were trained in using the two-sided documents, and proposed to include a training component in the outsourcing contract proposed by Xerox MPS.

Figure 7.1 describes the architecture of the co-creation effort conducted during the Assess and Optimize engagement of Xerox at the large chemical company described in the rest of this chapter.

They had demonstrated there was value to the project. The next step was to decide on how they were going to share it.

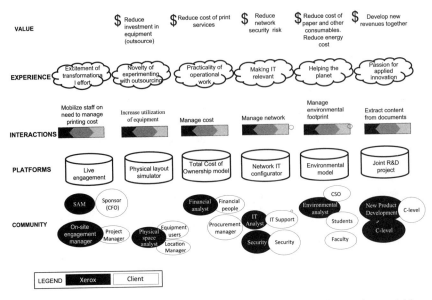

Fig. 7.1 Value Co-Creation map of Xerox with its customer. This chart is also available at http://www.eccpartnership.com/the-co-creation-edge.html

6 *With Data in Hand, Demonstrate that the Project Will Have a Good Return*

For SAMs and senior buyers, the size of the project is generally proportional to the size of the value that is anticipated as a result of the project for the customer firm. Psychologically, most firms try to visualize the benefit they expect to receive, and try to relate this to the dollar investment in the proposed project. The most common way to relate the two is to compute a breakeven time, e.g., how many months or years will it take for the project to pay for itself? SAMs associated with firms that provide immediate cost reduction products, or services such as Xerox MPS, can often design projects that pay for themselves in the first year, while SAMs in firms dealing with more capital-intensive industrial products typically have to allow more time before their customer can fully recover the value of their investment. ROI computations are also a popular way to relate benefits and project investment.

As we've already seen, a frequent bias of people looking at those computations is to overvalue the cost reduction benefits and to undervalue the revenue generating benefits. Overcoming this bias at the time of closing is often the difference between a narrow, cost-focused project, and a broader, more transformational project that values growth in revenues. Great SAMs and senior buyers know to sell both the cost reduction AND the revenue-generating agenda to their respective firm, which allows them to design and sell larger projects than people who live only in the cost reduction world. Experience also shows that decision makers frequently cluster into "operational buyers" purchasing cost reduction, and "strategic buyers" who like the idea of having a revenue or innovation component in the new relationship, and you need to win both to secure large projects. The best way to secure a go-ahead is to have both the strategic and operational factions on your side at the crucial moment.

At our chemical company, the site-based analysis was conducted on three sites (two plants and central headquarters office) and eventually extrapolated to the entire global network of plants and offices of the chemical company. The Assess and Optimize team had identified a total document production cost base of about $250 million globally (a combination of the opportunity costs of keeping the investment tied to document production on the chemical company's books, and operating costs). Through the use of the detailed analysis at the three sites, Xerox and the chemical company jointly demonstrated they could save about 20% of that cost for the chemical company. This suggested a cost reduction of $50 million per year was possible for the whole firm, which was validated by all the internal "stream leads" at the chemical company. The SAM proposed to the senior buyer a $50 million project that would have the project pay for itself the first year.

The senior buyer dismissed this initial proposal out of hand as too high. But the negotiation had started.

7 Agree on a Negotiation Process and Close

Negotiation of the final contract is undoubtedly an important interaction in the life of the SAM and the senior buyer. Much has been written about the psychology of deal-making: whom to bring with you and how to behave in closing meetings, or how to extract the last dollar in the transaction. There is a bit of poker-playing involved in the closing stages of a contract, and there are, therefore, skills which are helpful to have, but in our experience, 95% of closing success is driven by everything that has preceded the final negotiation process, and only 5% by the final *mano-a-mano* negotiation.

Ultimately, the negotiation leverage of the SAM and the senior buyer is a function of what constitutes the next best alternative for each of them.

If you have successfully reached stage four of the relationship-building process, the next best alternative should be either the unattractive "do nothing" (at which point the company gives up on the benefits opportunity), or the unequally unattractive option of going to another company that will offer a pale transactional copy of what you're been collaboratively building so patiently with your partner, which means they will have to redo everything you've already done with the first company, and your organization will not understand why they have to do the work twice. So if you're trying to become a great negotiator, you'd better learn how to create leverage by implementing the relationship-building we describe in this book (the 95%) rather than try to become the next Donald Trump (the 5%).[11]

The best design for the final negotiation process involves having the SAM and the senior buyer agree *a priori* on the process they will follow in the closing: who will be involved on which side (it is in everybody's interest to narrow down that group as much as possible); how many meetings will be conducted (the fewer, the better); what is the deadline at which the process will conclude (you need to have a deadline to avoid negotiating for the next two years); and how the contract-writing process will unfold after that (to ensure that the legal side does not turn into a problem once the negotiation has concluded).

A big part of the negotiation, of course, has to do with the ultimate price of the contract. All the way through stages three and four of the relationship-building process, SAMs and senior buyers should qualify each other on the expected price, guaranteeing that the two parties are at least in the same ball park.

At the chemical company, the final negotiation process proved reasonably uneventful. The Xerox SAM and the chemical company senior buyer agreed they were going to have three meetings within a week. The first one is the one where the SAM proposed a $50 million project that the senior buyer found excessive. The SAM asked the senior buyer which part of the business case that was presented, the chemical company did not want to pursue (and, therefore, which part of the project ought to be cut). It turns out the whole company wanted the entire project to go ahead as is, but had only budgeted for only about 70% of the proposed cost. The SAM went back to his team and suggested in a second meeting how the cost of the project could be brought down if some of the supervisory services that Xerox was outsourc-

---

[11] See Donald Trump and Tony Schwartz, the Art of the Deal, 2004, Ballantine Books.

ing could stay within the responsibility of the chemical firm. They settled on a project costing $40 million a year. A third and final meeting confirmed the agreement, leading to applause on both sides and the pouring of champagne in the board room.

They now had a contract. The SAM and senior buyer invited their respective teams to a team dinner in the best restaurant in town and celebrated.

8 Celebrate and Start Recruiting the Right People for the Delivery Phase

Celebrating the signing of a major sales or procurement contract is a healthy tradition. SAMs and senior buyers should never hesitate to host such events by inviting their teams to dinners, or other forms of entertainment, to thank them for all the hard work they have done, and to show them that their work is appreciated. These events are moments of pure joy, or exuberance, full of anecdotes and memories about the highs and lows of the courtship leading to the contract. These moment of celebration, in addition to providing a nice fun episode in the life of the team, also profoundly shape the culture of the future partnership, showing whether some true intimacy has been created between the two teams, or whether the relationship remains mostly of a functional, business nature.

While closing a major contract is a significant accomplishment worthy of celebration, the SAM's and senior buyer's attention must turn immediately, after the conclusion of the sale and procurement contract, to the delivery phase of the contract. Job one is to secure the right people on each side; it's never too early to begin the process of recruiting the staff for delivery. The people best qualified to handle the delivery challenge are often the people who participated in the contract design work in the first place, first, because they know both organizations, and second, because they understand how the identified value now needs to be delivered. There are, of course, multiple reasons why the people involved in the contract development stage cannot stay with the delivery team, either because they have to go sell or procure somewhere else, or because they have to return to their functional duties in finance, or environmental affairs, rather than forever participate in special projects. Either way, there is a need for a new influx of talent for delivery.

The transition from sale to delivery is often accompanied by some tension on the feasibility of delivering what has been sold. It is not uncommon for delivery people to blame the sales team for having overpromised, making the project difficult or impossible to deliver. There is often a cultural gap between the selling and the delivery team, which the SAM and the senior buyer have to bridge. Selling teams often are like the Marines: they help SAMs take the hill, win the contract and move on to their next battle. Delivery teams are like the Army: they stay with projects for years and have to build long-term relationships while producing, not promising, results. The typical tension that arises has the Marines thinking of the Army as a slow and uninspired infantry, while the infantry views the Marines as flashy and over-promising, leaving them to repair the land after some of the devastation that occurred when taking the hill.

Because the role of the modern SAM and senior buyer extends far beyond the moment of sale and procurement, they have a key role to play in ensuring continuity, making sure their company recruits the right people for the project, and introducing those people to their counterpart organizations.

At the chemical company, the transition proved reasonably smooth. Xerox had introduced some of the delivery people in the last three weeks of the Assess and Optimize phase of work, allowing the chemical company to see the new, future leader of the delivery project in action. He had played a gradually more visible role on the project, so that by the time of the final presentation, he was already providing a quiet reassurance that the team getting in place could deliver the promised benefits. Two prominent members of the Assess and Optimize team of Xerox were also built into the project budget for another two months, ensuring that there would be a good transition to delivery. The chemical company's staff expressed a bit of nervousness about the massive changing of the guard, but took solace in the fact that the SAM personally committed that the delivery team would be of first grade quality.

"I'm not going anywhere", he promised, using the trust he had built as guarantee of more good things to come.

9   Put in Place the Value-Tracking Mechanism for the Delivery Phase of Work

The next chapter in this book is dedicated to the value capture stage that comes after the signing of a major contract; we will not describe it here in great length, except to say that one of the key roles of the SAM and the senior buyer is to put in place, immediately after the sale, the process through which value will be captured and communicated in the delivery phase. In most cases, there is already a platform in place gathering data across the two companies, often accompanied by some kind of "war room" where those results are shared and where the joint team meets. Because of the relative brevity of the relationship-building process up to that point, the platform is typically rustic at best and the war room mostly *ad hoc*. Delivery requires putting in place a more institutional platform, which requires important start-up activities on the financial and IT side, while other people attend to the communication aspect of that value (how frequently will we report, and in what form).

In our chemical company example, Xerox and its client appointed a start-up team charged with these activities, with a mandate to have everything in pace within two months. It took them a bit longer, but after a few hiccups, everything fell in place quickly.

10 Start Working on the Next Opportunity the First Morning After Closing

High performing SAMs and senior buyers know that the sale marks only the beginning of the relationship. In a truly co-creative relationship, both continuously surface new opportunities for each other during the relationship-building phase and they recognize that there are many other opportunities they can go after together. Because one cannot tackle all problems at once, they focus on what can be contracted for in the short-term, but share with each other that there may be further opportunities in their relationship. It is, in fact, a sign of a healthy relationship that the two partners, even in the throes of a major negotiation, start pointing out future opportunities to each other.

In the case of our chemical company, the Xerox SAM and the senior buyer knew that the major document production outsourcing contract they first signed opened the door to Xerox providing deeper process outsourcing services in document- and regulation-intensive processes. They expected at the time that Xerox would soon be able to parlay its document management process expertise into content services, whereby Xerox would start managing some reporting processes on behalf of the chemical company. This is, in fact, what happened and the relationship between the two firms has steadily grown over the last few years, producing a new wave of sales for Xerox, and cost reductions and improved efficiency at the chemical company.

In this chapter, we reviewed the commitment part of the relationship-building process and how the two parties finalize value and close the deal. We now turn to "the morning after", the moment where the two companies start working together to capture the value they have identified in the contract they just signed.

CHAPTER 8

The Long-Term Relationship: Deliver and Document Value

I t is the morning after. The SAM has celebrated the sale with her team, and the senior buyer has toasted the new procurement contract. But reality soon sets in; there is a lot of work to be done on both sides. The most immediate task is to carry out all the start-up activities linked to the new contract, with its cohort of transition issues, such as making sure the departing "selling" team shares everything it knows with the delivery team, under the vigilant eye of the procurement team that wants to make sure the supplier is not pulling a bait-and-switch scheme with the A team leaving and being replaced by a B team. It is time for a new phase in the relationship-building process, the fifth and next-to-last phase in our chronology. The pace slows down a little from the frantic rhythm of the final days preceding the contract. The sprinters are replaced by long-distance runners on both sides. The emphasis is now on delivering the value that has been promised and on documenting that value.

In our human metaphor, we are now in the long-term relationship phase that follows the commitment made to each other. After the celebration of the new union comes the reality of living together. Now that all family members and friends have left, the two partners look at each other with some anxiety and have to put in place the practical aspects of living together. Both hope that the promise of their early life together blossoms into a blissful reality that includes sharing a physical place and common resources.

In the long-term relationship stage of our process, the ten phases of the co-creation cycle again morph into a different form:

1. Create a deep, granular definition of the opportunity areas and identify the stream of benefits resulting from each of them.
2. Train the teams that own the delivery of the promised benefits and help them become committed to delivering the identified benefits.
3. Engage global delivery teams through a common value-measurement mechanism.
4. Construct an analytical performance model for each benefits area.
5. Build and install an interactive or real-time value measurement platform.
6. Compute value created in each area, aggregate total value, and hypothesize new ways to create value.
7. Use the quarterly or yearly performance review to communicate value created.
8. Role-model the value creation philosophy in the personal relationship between SAM and senior buyer.
9. Increase scope and risk of value to go after. Potentially create a formal value-sharing mechanism.
10. Build a value expansion plan.

In this chapter, we shall use the case of SKF, the large Swedish multinational, best known for its industrial bearings used in machines that have rotating equipment of any kind. It calls itself "the knowledge engineering" company.[1] The "knowledge engineering" approach refers to the fact that SKF, in its more than 100-year history, has been gradually moving up the value chain: from selling components, to providing assemblies, to supplying systems, and today, developing entire solutions that include hardware, software and services for the entire lifecycle of the machine the SKF product is a part of.

---

[1] See SKF web site for description of basic concept: http://www.skf.com/group/our-company/the-power-of-knowledge-engineering/index.html. There is also a short video headlining the approach: https://www.youtube.com/watch?v=cOJ-2l9tVPQ. A slightly more complete description of the philosophy can be found at: http://www.slideshare.net/vinnovase/begg-bilder.

SKF had total sales of $8.5 billion in 2014 and earned a respectable 13.9% return on capital employed during that same year.[2] The company sells to 40 different industries: from aerospace to automotive, process industries, energy, and food and beverage companies. Here, we will focus more specifically on how it builds relationships with its pulp and paper customers, and we will zero in on its use of a process and platform called the Documented Solutions Program (DSP), that tracks the value SKF creates for its customers.

1   Create a Deep, Granular Definition of the Opportunity Areas and Identify the Stream of Benefits Resulting from Each of Them

By now, what you originally identified as problem areas you wanted to tackle have morphed into opportunity areas, specifically itemized in the contract you just signed. You also have a new team on the ground on both the supplier and the customer side, and chances are that you have many new players on both sides who did not participate in the contract negotiation. Prepare for them to be highly skeptical of the feasibility of capturing the value in the exact form that it is framed in the contract. Delivery people on the supplier side will be tempted to blame the sales people for over promising, thereby creating some wiggle room for themselves if delivering the intended benefits falls a bit short. On the customer side, people charged with delivery will similarly suggest that the procurement folks were over-sold on the anticipated benefits, hoping them to create some breathing room of their own. This is where the SAM and senior buyer need to partner effectively to keep everybody honest by coaching their respective sides on what needs to be achieved during the pre-contract and the post-contract phase.

Up to the end of phase four in the relationship-building cycle, the analytical work could only go so far. This is because the two partners had not yet committed to each other, which imposed confidentiality restrictions on the exchange of information. Also the supplier could not afford to delve too deeply in too many areas, because there had not yet been a significant commitment of resources on the part of the supplier. For these reasons, once the delivery of the project begins in phase five, it is helpful to revisit the exact nature of the problems the two companies want to address. As we shall see in the next section, participating in this conceptualization of the problem, and

---

[2] See 2014 annual report: a PDF version can be found at http://www.skf.com/irassets/afw/files/press/skf/SKF-Annual-Report-2014-150308-Fast.pdf.

the modeling of benefits slated to accrue, will also help the new members of the team develop ownership of the problem and allow its eventual resolution. If they are part of the model-building, they are more likely to commit to its implementation.

When SKF sells a project to a pulp and paper company, the business case is typically articulated around the value that the new product and its associated services will create throughout the life of the product.[3] The idea is to show that while the product may appear expensive at the outset, the Total Cost of Ownership (or TCO) is dramatically lower over the life of the asset because of the quality of SKF's products. The company sometimes makes this argument with the metaphor of a "priceberg",[4] which shows that while customers often only view the visible part of the iceberg (the price of the new equipment and services), the true cost lies in the submerged part of the "priceberg", which comprises all the hidden costs of the part breaking down, the hassle of sourcing and replacing it under emergency conditions, missing out on production and generally disrupting the flow of operations at the plant.

This, of course, is a conceptual argument that many buyers tend to go "yea, yea, yea" to, before asking for a significant price reduction with a renewed vigor. This is where a more analytical formulation of the problem is needed, and the involvement of technical users of the machine is helpful. It is time to go beyond the "bigger than a breadbox" estimates from the pre-sale phases, and build a bottom-up view of where the hidden value is located. Here is how the SKF sales and service team, under the general leadership of the SAM, approaches the issue of creating that granular view of the problem areas and the opportunities they contain.

Many things can be optimized on a paper machine, and the SKF team knows where the levers of profitability lie, based on the preliminary work that has already taken place before the sale, as well as through their own experience. Their first task is to identify the drivers of profitability for each specific machine, build a list of problems and opportunities, and encourage their

---

[3] The life cycle management practiced by SKF for machine tools is described for example on the company website at: http://www.skf.com/us/industry-solutions/machine-tool/life-cycle-management/index.html.

[4] For a complete description of the SKF "priceberg" and Total Cost of Ownership approaches, see presentation made by Todd Snelgrove, Global manager, Value at MyPurchasingCenter.com webcast on April 10, 2013: http://www.mypurchasingcenter.com/files/4513/6560/7741/Purch_-_4-13_Pres_no_builds.pdf.

counterpart in the customer plant to become motivated to address the issues that limit the machine's performance. And there are many.

Whether for printing or packaging applications, paper machines are big, capital-intensive units that can theoretically produce paper 365 days a year, 24 hours a day. Of course, it does not quite work that way in reality, so any gap between real-life production and this theoretical potential is fair game for SKF and the SAM to go after. First, machines break down unexpectedly (this is euphemistically referred to as "unscheduled maintenance"). The rotating parts of paper machines are particularly vulnerable because of the conditions in which they work; they have to endure water in the front part of the machine where wood-chip based pulp and water are combined with additives to form the paper; they then tolerate high heat as the paper is channeled through successive ovens, and cope with high speeds throughout the process.

The name of the game in paper production is to maximize output by getting the machines to run at the highest possible speed, but without triggering incidents where the giant paper roll on the machine rips down in the middle of the run, or creates winding problems on the rollers, such that the machine needs to be stopped and restarted. And of course, the higher the speed, the more likely the machine is to develop problems, such as having parts that vibrate to the point where they break down, or require massive amounts of costly lubrication just for the machine to stay cool. In the end, paper machines are like NASCAR or Formula 1 cars that continuously strive for extreme performance, but are always on the brink of crashing into a wall. Keeping them on the track is where SKF comes in.

And there is more. One of the pesky problems in paper-making involves changing over from one product for one customer to a second product for another customer. The time involved in this transition is wasted production time. Minimizing this changeover time is, therefore, another major reservoir of productivity for the SKF SAM and his team, and the bearings, lubrication services and on-line monitoring systems offered by SKF can play an important role in minimizing this transition time.

There are also specific problems the SKF team can help address in the finishing area. Finishing involves using slitting machines that take the giant rolls produced by the paper machine and cut them to width and length, to create the finished product that the customer can buy as either (narrower) rolls, or sheets. There again, the machines used in finishing contain SKF parts that have a high impact on the quality of the rolls (e.g., in avoiding bad wind-ups that will jam later as the customer prints on them) or the sheets (ensuring they are homogeneous and can be processed at high speed by the customer).

Once these areas have been identified, the SKF service team then moves to engage the customer team in the pursuit of identified opportunities .

2   Train the Teams that Own the Delivery of the Promised Benefits and Help them Become Committed to Delivering the Identified Benefits

Because the cast of characters usually changes from pre-sale to post-sale on both sides, the SAM and senior buyer have to create the required continuity. Their job is to take each of the identified problem/opportunity areas and, just like they did in the pre-sale phases, assemble a (new) joint team that will undertake the responsibility for delivering the benefits associated with each area. Large, transformational projects can have as many as nine or ten different teams participating in the delivery, and they typically report to a steering committee made of executives of both companies, with the SAM and senior buyer acting both as coordinators of the stream teams and as liaisons to the Steering Committee.

There is a subtle psychology involved on the part of the SAM and senior buyer in this phase. On the one hand, they can invoke the power of the contract that has just been signed and point to the fact that senior management on both sides "signed on" to the benefits stipulated in the contract. The implied message is: you do not want to be caught disagreeing with the views of your senior management. On the other hand, every owner of a problem or opportunity has to be convinced that the benefits are indeed present in their area (. This requires house-to-house fighting on the part of the SAM and the senior buyer, and sometimes requires calling back the person who, inside the sales team, built the benefits case before the sale.

When SKF works to improve the profitability of a paper machine, the first port of call is operations. Hierarchically, the operations area involves at least two levels: there is typically a paper machine superintendent (or equivalent title) responsible for the overall supervision of the asset, and the actual production is managed by highly-skilled operators who work in shifts and run the machine day and night. Delivering the benefits promised by the SKF SAM requires the political support of the superintendent, but success depends on convincing the individual operators to start working differently. For example, operators are most likely to notice vibration noise developing in an area, or small wrinkles forming in the paper, typical predictors of upcoming problems.

The other main set of actors in any SKF project in the paper industry is the maintenance team charged with keeping the machine running through a combination of scheduled maintenance (the good kind, because it is less costly and is designed to anticipate and avoid problems) and unscheduled maintenance (the undesirable kind, because it happens in scramble mode and steals valuable time from production).

In addition, quality and engineering in the paper plant often also play an indirect role in SKF projects, because quality issues are often traced back to machine issues (e.g., uneven winding of the rolls) and engineering is charged with designing major modifications of production equipment and processes. And of course, financial people frequently become involved to validate the accounting of benefits accruing from SKF's work.

SAMs and senior buyers have to orchestrate this multi-team process, not only at the level of a single paper machine in a given plant, but at the consolidated level of each plant, which will typically have multiple machines, and eventually at the level of an entire global paper company with its plants on multiple continents. When one realizes that paper companies are increasingly competing with each other on a planetary scale, one can measure the true challenge of getting teams organized and setting up a value-tracking mechanism that supports them for the entire worldwide manufacturing network that the SKF SAM and the senior buyer in the paper company are responsible for.

Setting teams up is the easy part, when compared to actually running them.

3   Engage Global Delivery Teams Through a Common Value-Measurement Mechanism

It used to be that pulp and paper companies had global "learning", or "center of excellence" initiatives at the corporate level, charged with orchestrating the exchange of best practices across global plants. There used to be meetings where the Scandinavian operations or maintenance staff met its Brazilian, American and Asian equivalent and exchanged tips on what they had learned. Today, the profitability pressure in the pulp and paper industry, as in most other industries, has increased to the point where initiatives of this type have largely disappeared, because of their cost, creating a knowledge void that companies are trying to fill through other means.

Suppliers are increasingly being asked to fill this void and to hide the costly knowledge dissemination process they run inside the price they charge for their products and services. Because suppliers are asked to play a greater role in identifying productivity opportunities and teaching their customers how to harvest these opportunities, suppliers, led by the SAM, have to become effective facilitators of global teams, simultaneously pursuing similar opportunities in multiple geographies. The role of the senior buyer is to hold the SAM and his team accountable for effectively managing this global team process.

The problem with global teams is that the value they bring is often hard to measure, which is why most companies have given up on running them. What suppliers can provide is a hard backbone to the team process by building a global value measurement mechanism that links every purchase of equipment by the customer to some form of identifiable, bottom-line benefits. The idea is to make the value documentation process the killer app for the global network, engendering migration of ideas from one geography to the other, encouraging the sale of more equipment in new parts of the world for the supplier, and allowing the customer to create increasingly greater performance improvements. At its best, the value-tracking mechanism encourages local teams to compete with each other in the pursuit of new opportunities, allowing a fast migration of best practices.

As an illustration of this thinking, SKF has instituted a highly-acclaimed process called the Documented Solutions Program (DSP), which is the foundation of its strategic account management program. The company defines DSP as "a tool that allows the SAM and his team to find opportunities, to measure the expected benefits involved, to prioritize the opportunities, to implement them, to measure actual results obtained, and to replicate the approach elsewhere in the company's network".[5] From the customer's standpoint, DSP helps the customer justify the purchase from SKF. From SKF's perspective, it accelerates the sales cycle by invoking the documented ROI of previous projects.

---

[5] Presentation made by Tom Johnstone, (then) CEO of SKF at SAMA's 50th anniversary conference on May 22–29, 2014 in Orlando, Florida. This proprietary SAMA presentation may be made available on request from SAMA.

So what does DSP actually consist of? It is a simple input-output model that allows an SKF service person to interview an operations and maintenance person in a paper plant, and share some simple characteristics of the machine, the production it runs, the production environment in which it operates, and some cost numbers. These input variables are then entered into the model, compared to benchmarks in a central database, and generate an estimate of the productivity improvement that can be expected given certain equipment-related actions the software suggests.

Individual DSP results become the foundation for the sale (using expected results), but also for the tracking of value actually created (using actual results). The DSP allows both the SAM and the senior buyer to develop a common language they can use to further strengthen their relationship. For SKF, it is a source of competitive advantage, because few of its competitors have a savings documentation process as sophisticated as SKF's. For the senior buyer, this gives him analytical legitimacy in claiming benefits when challenged by operational areas or top management.

Of course, SKF had to invest significant resources in order to develop the DSP process to the point where it is today, starting with the building of a performance model for a single paper-making machine.

4   Create an Analytical Performance Model for Each Benefits Area

Once you are committed to building a global value documentation system, your first task is to build the mechanics of the system and avoid the garbage-in-garbage-out syndrome. World-class value tracking models start at the micro-level of single machines or service areas, and then aggregate the model from there all the way to worldwide savings and revenue opportunities. A value documentation model is a representation of the mental map of the most knowledgeable people in a given area on what actions cause what effects. The traditional way to build such a model is for a set of experts to create it for one representative unit in the network (say, a particular machine or plant), test it against reality at that unit, then generalize and adapt the model that has been built to similar units elsewhere. In this approach, the experts formulate the hypothesis on how things work, then test whether they were right, and if they were, attempt to generalize the model.

As we have already seen, there is another, more leading-edge way of figuring out what causes drive what effects. It involves "discovering" the model from actual data that the machines collect automatically, then trying to figure out what correlates with what using a combination of expert-driven hypotheses and software-driven analytics. This second approach is often referred to as Machine-to-Machine dialog, or the Internet of Things. In many industries, physical objects collect more and more data through built-in sensors, transmit this data through a gateway (electronic communication device and protocol) to a cloud server where massive amount of data is analyzed and distilled into prescriptions for action using a logic sequence called an algorithm.

SKF has long been a pioneer in the more traditional, expert-driven approach to value documentation through its DSP process, but, as we shall see later, it is also developing an Internet of Things approach for some of its customers. For now, the model works in the following fashion[6]:

Modeling at the machine level starts by stating the theoretical maximum output of a paper machine in a given week (24 hours a week, 7 days a week, or 168 hours per week). It then deducts from this total theoretical amount the scheduled downtime of the machine for maintenance, inviting the question of whether the amount of scheduled maintenance can be reduced and, if so, how. This leaves the paper company with a reduced time available for production. The next reduction in that production time comes from unscheduled losses (which SKF then tries to minimize through various equipment-related preventive actions, such as replacing old equipment with newer equipment, thereby increasing uptime) and from potential excess capacity in the market. In the current environment, packaging paper typically always finds a customer, thereby making any "de-bottlenecking" of the machine usable to produce more and generate more margin, but print paper suffers from excess capacity globally, so capacity increases do not automatically translate in additional sales and margin. The model also measures reductions in productive time coming from speed losses, which the system further breaks down into operator skills, equipment or lubrication issues, and quality losses, when the paper produced does not meet the original specification and needs to be sold as scrap. The model we just described constitutes the high-level architecture of the computation. There is, of course, a lot more detail associated with each area of the paper machine, and each action that can be undertaken to mitigate

---

[6] See technical brochure entitled *SKF paper machine optimization: Increasing overall machine efficiency and productivity.* This brochure can be downloaded at http://www.skf.com/binary/30-125610/Paper-machine-optimization_10054EN.pdf.

some of the losses. SKF's strength lies in the fact that it is able to train its own people on the model, and uses it to train its customers on best practices in managing a paper machine.

So far, we have focused on the design of the model itself. Let us now turn to how the data is actually collected and utilized once the model has been designed.

5   Build and Install an Interactive or a Real-Time Value Measurement Platform

For many years, suppliers created a presale business case without ever tracking the benefits they actually delivered after the sale. Under pressure from customers, the next generation of value-tracking systems involved building a war room, where data was manually aggregated and analyzed at periodic intervals of time, then plastered on the walls of the war room to invite a dialog with visitors interested in the project underway. In a third generation, war rooms then started using more and more sophisticated technology-based visualization technologies and began to rely on data fed directly to the tracking system from the major enterprise IT systems of the firm. Today, the most sophisticated value-measurement systems rely on real-life data captured automatically by sensor-equipped physical objects as part of day-to-day operations. This data is then sent to the cloud and analyzed by a central group that uses a combination of old-fashioned analysis and some of the newest analytics techniques provided by Internet of Things software. As already mentioned, the most sophisticated companies not only measure value in this fashion, but attempt to discover new value creation patterns between the variables being measured, thereby constantly figuring out new ways to improve operations.

SKF offers an example of such a sophisticated real-time system that not only measures value through a host of operational variables on the paper-making machine, but also acts as a decision-support system that offers a customized, monitor-based presentation of that data for each decision-maker, from paper machine superintendent, product manager (who cares about quality and volume), operators at various stages of the machine and maintenance people. As stated in the promotional literature of SKF,[7] "it provides a

---

[7] See technical brochure entitled: Proactive Reliability Maintenance, available at http://www.skf.com/binary/77-38475/PRM-Brochure.pdf.

dynamic resource for machine and process diagnosis, analysis, reporting and corrective action."

The beauty of the system is that it removes all the tedium of data collection from managers and employees, as the data is automatically collected by the equipment and stored on a server where it can be analyzed. Think of this as an SKF bearing that measures its own vibration, speed, load, or temperature, regulates its own lubrication flow, speaks to the electric engine nearby, as well as to the moving flatbed carrying the paper, and the drums that will make it into rolls at the end of the machine. Today, SKF is able to generate operational prescriptions for all these pieces individually for the benefit of the people in charge of maintaining or operating the equipment.

The documentation of the value created by recent sales of equipment and services is what keeps the relationship going with its customers, making it the first order of business for both SAM and senior buyer.

6   Compute Value Created in Each Area, Aggregate Total Value, and Hypothesize New Ways to Create Value

The best sales argument a SAM will ever have to make the next sale is proof that previous sales generated a good return for the customer. Similarly, the most value-added contribution a senior buyer can make is not that he lowered the purchase price of the product bought, but that he reduced the total cost of ownership of that product. Of course, demonstrating that in convincing fashion is the main challenge for both the SAM and senior buyer, and it requires a lot of systems infrastructure and work.

We saw in the previous section how the tracking of benefits has improved through successive generations to become an on-line, live decision-support system in the most advanced form. Even when such systems are in place, the SAM and senior buyer still have to carry out two tasks: aggregating the value created in various parts of the customer's global network, and figuring out new ways to create value. Aggregating value is an important, often missing, step. Suppliers are generally ahead of customers when it comes to putting in place systems that allow global computations of this type, so the SAM can use this ability to compute aggregated savings numbers for competitive advantage, and to convince the customer to continue giving the SAM more business.

The ultimate value of a good tracking system lies in the ability to use demonstrated results to create credibility for the exploration of new ways to create value. Having a demonstrated record of value creation will earn you the right to propose new projects and will encourage the customer to want to test your new product or system if it makes such a claim. Senior buyers buy from SAMs they trust, and trust gives you the right to experiment at the edge of the known value creation path. World-class SAMs and senior buyers strive to have a portfolio where tried and true value-creating projects represent around 80–90% of their portfolio, but they make a point of reserving 10–20% of their portfolio for innovative, more experimental projects whose value is less known or deterministic, but that can create new pathways to value creation. Internet of Things projects generally fall into this category of more experimental projects.

As of December 2013, SKF's Documented Solutions Program (DSP) had developed 47,230 verified use cases of its equipment and services.[8] It was tracking value in 25 end-use or industry applications (heavy industry is one of them) and 120 industry sub-segments (such as pulp and paper-making). It had demonstrated that SKF created $4.2 billion worth of value, by codifying 142 different solution packages, with completed analyses described in six languages. The work was done with 34 global accounts involving a SAM, and seven of those were in the pulp and paper industry.

Until recently, the intelligence was still principally located in the brains of the SKF engineers and its customers, but SKF is developing an Internet of Things approach where the pattern of developing variables measured by the machines can automatically generate algorithm-based prescriptions, which users can then apply. For example, SKF recently announced it has developed an Internet of Things technology called SKF Insight that allows a large wind turbine manufacturer to anticipate the maintenance requirements of its equipment, a particularly valuable feature given the cost of servicing machines often located in remote, hostile environments.[9]

---

[8] Presentation made by Tom Johnstone, (then) CEO of SKF at SAMA's 50th anniversary conference on May 22–29, 2014 in Orlando, Florida. This proprietary SAMA presentation may be made available on request from SAMA.
[9] See SKF announcement at http://www.skf.com/group/news-and-media/news-search/2015-04-13_skf_insight_intelligent_bearing_technology_trialed_in_railway_and_wind_energy_sectors.html.

7   Use the Quarterly or Yearly Performance Review to Communicate Value Created

Periodically, the SAM and the senior buyer sit together for a review of recent performance and set goals for the next period. Most businesses hold such meetings on a quarterly basis, and price reviews usually take place once a year. These meetings are key to the life of the relationship between SAM and senior buyer, because each quarterly business review represents a potential inflection point in the sales-procurement curve where SAM and senior buyer can decide to increase the amount of business they do together, or reduce the scope of the relationship.

SKF uses its Documented Solutions Program as an important tool in the quarterly business reviews its SAMs participate in. In some accounts, there is a live, interactive system in place that measures value. In the majority of cases, the SAM simply collaborates with members of the local sales and service teams attached to each plant to work with their local counterpart at the supplier to compute value numbers for the quarterly, or yearly, business review and compare that to SKF-supplied benchmarks.

The quarterly, and even more so, the yearly price review are intense moments for the SAM and senior buyer alike. Most importantly, they drive the feeling of self-worth for the SAM and senior buyer.

8   Role-Model the Value Creation Philosophy in the Personal Relationship Between SAM and Senior Buyer

One of the main goals of the co-creation approach is to break the confrontational win-lose relationship that often exists at the outset between the SAM and the senior buyer. Absent any documentation of value of the type advocated for in this chapter, negotiating on price and terms becomes the default position for the senior buyer, which in turn makes the SAM's job miserable. The SAM is then left with no alternative, but to try to bypass the senior buyer and seek to sell directly to more technical buyers elsewhere in the supplier's system. This further antagonizes the senior buyer who is then tempted to retaliate by threatening the SAM with marginalization if she continues to try to escape the grip of the procurement department. This is the vicious circle of classic arm-twisting negotiation.

When there is a value documentation system in place, SAMs and senior buyers become natural allies. There is still a hard negotiation to be conducted between them periodically, but both are in a position to document to their respective organization (and to each other's organization) that their relationship is on solid ground, showing there is real value created, and their relationship is not the result of some random friendship they may have struck together. Going into a review with solid value numbers makes the SAM confident that she is not rolling the dice at every meeting. It also allows the senior buyer to feel that he will be able to justify his choice of supplier without being suspected of playing an arbitrary power game whereby he distributes the "goodies" to people he likes. There is a trend at SKF to increasingly recruit SAMs who are able to convey that long-term value creation is what SKF is about.[10] Over the last fifteen years, ever since SKF started its major drive toward measuring total cost of ownership and lifecycle value of its products and services, SAMs have increasingly been recruited from the population of people who understand value analysis, giving preference, for example, to people with a background in vibration analysis to people with a more traditional sales background.

9   *Increase Scope and Risk of Value to Go After: Potentially Create a Formal Value-Sharing Mechanism*

Once the SAM and senior buyer have developed the intimacy that accrues from generating documented value together, they can move on to an exploration of new opportunities for value creation. The first place to go is areas adjacent to the ones where they already have a shared track record, such as applying the same approach at other plants, or geographies facing similar problems. Or it may include venturing into new territories altogether, either because the supplier faces pesky issues that the senior buyer thinks could call on the capabilities of the SAM's organization, or because the supplier has new ideas, products or services that the SAM thinks might be useful in the supplier's organization.

As the amount of value created by two partners together grows, one of the two partners may want to change the business model between the two firms and suggest a value-sharing arrangement. In a value-sharing arrangement, the supplier stops charging for equipment and services by pricing each product or service individually, but undertakes contractual responsibility for delivering a

---

[10] Interview of Corrado Cesti, Head of Heavy Industry, SKF Group.

certain amount of bottom-line value for its customer and is compensated as a percentage of that value.

As in anything else, there are advantages and drawbacks associated with a value-sharing system. On the positive side, the supplier can create a model that escapes the tyranny of the cost-plus system, where the cost of its products and services is reverse-engineered by the procurement department of the customer and its price constrained by the margin allowed by the customer on top of that cost. In a value-sharing system, cost and revenue become disconnected, potentially allowing greater profitability. From the customer standpoint, this places a portion of the delivery risk squarely on the shoulders of the supplier by making the payment proportional to the value actually delivered.

The downside of value-sharing arrangement lies in three areas:

1. the volatility of value outcomes
2. the complexity of the system required to measure value
3. the difficulty of determining who deserves credit for creating the value between supplier and customer.

On the value itself, it is one thing to try to document value to justify the next sale or procurement contract, but quite another to make the amount of the revenue indexed in some fashion to the measurement of that value. The volatility risk in a value-sharing arrangement can be daunting to both supplier (risk of not getting paid anywhere near the cost of the equipment and services in case of failure to deliver the benefits) and customer (ending up paying much more than a traditional transaction would have warranted, because the measured benefits turn out to be huge). When a value measurement system starts being used to compute payments made by the supplier firm, the amount of rigor required increases exponentially, because the temptation for one party or the other to game the system increases. Building a truly objective measurement system can prove to be too daunting a task for both parties. Finally, value delivery success requires that both supplier and customer create common value together as an integrated team, but value-sharing arrangements force the drawing of a line between what is attributable to the actions of the supplier and of the customer, which is inherently divisive.

In SKF's case, for example, should a reduction in machine downtime in a given plant be attributed to the better bearings, better lubrication system, or excellent monitoring system and training put in place by the SKF team, or is it due to the fact that the plant superintendent and the operators of the paper plant launched a new preventive maintenance program that happens to use SKF equipment and services? The game can rapidly become destructive if plant personnel gets the feeling that SKF is claiming benefits that are legitimately theirs, and vice-versa, if SKF personnel starts feeling cheated out of value it thinks was created by them rather than the plant's personnel. All that matters in the end is that the two parties work together closely to achieve the benefits. For all these reasons, SKF has so far preferred staying with a more traditional pricing scheme, and using the Documented Solutions Program as the backbone and rationale for the price it asks for.

Once the value system is in place, the next step is to start visualizing where value will come from in the future.

10   Build a Value Expansion Plan

High-performing SAMs and senior buyers continuously strive to expand the scope of their value creation network, utilizing their shared track record to create new opportunities that they jointly decide to explore. There is a continuum of risk and reward that SAM and senior buyers contemplate, once they reach phase five in the relationship-building cycle, the subject of this chapter. The portfolio of opportunities they should create is a mix of short-term, mid-term and longer-term opportunities, each representing a different mix of risk and return (technology people sometimes refers to these as "three horizons"). The short-term projects are made up of fairly safe initiatives with predictable results, because they represent a migration from proven value-creation approaches already used elsewhere in the supplier's network. These constitute the bread-and-butter sales for the SAM and regular spend for the buyer. Mid-term projects are a little riskier and their ROI a little farther out, but the probability of value-creating success remains high. Finally, the long-term projects are more speculative in nature, less tested and riskier, but they may unlock significant new sources of value if successful.

The typical SKF SAM works with multiple time-to-benefit horizons and the value-tracking system needs to accommodate that dimension. She offers projects that have ROI of only a few months, for example, when analysis through the DSP computation establishes that replacing a particular bearing will immediately reduce unplanned downtime and protect valuable production hours worth several hundreds of thousands of dollars. She offers mid-

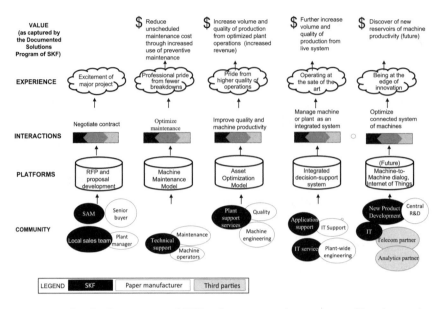

Fig. 8.1 Value Co-Creation map of SKF with its paper-making customer. This chart is also available at http://www.eccpartnership.com/the-co-creation-edge.html

term projects with time horizons of a year or two that aim, for example, to replace high-cost maintenance under fire with a lower-cost, preventive maintenance program that periodically replaces equipment on the basis of their average "mean time between failure". SKFs most innovative SAMs also spearhead the longer-term projects of the firm that involve implementing integrated decision-support systems across entire machines or plants, including placing multiple sensors at various stages of the paper-making machine that allow the creation of analytical insights and the development of new value creation insights using an Internet of Things or Machine-to-Machine approach.

Figure 8.1 summarizes how SKF generates value with its customers, as described throughout this chapter.

In this chapter, we saw how supplier and customer can team up to measure the value they create together and use the value documentation system as the backbone of their relationship. In the next chapter, we turn to how the two companies can gradually expand the value over time.

CHAPTER 9

The Family: Expand Value

In Chap. 8, we saw how to track and deliver value after the contract has been signed. In this chapter, we outline how the delivery of demonstrated benefits allows the relationship to grow beyond the initial project and develop into a multi-pronged relationship managed by the SAM and the senior buyer. In our human relationship metaphor, this is the equivalent of the two parents having children, who will themselves beget grandchildren and great grandchildren and continuously enlarge the tribe.

The ten steps of our co-creation cycle take a particular shape at this advanced stage in the relationship-building cycle:

1. Identify new problems whose resolution will change the business model of both firms and require significant investment.
2. Involve new players outside the two core firms in tackling the problem you have identified.
3. Agree on an IP sharing structure and governance process that engages the various sides and protects their interest.
4. Formulate specific hypotheses on where the business value will lie in the new mode of interaction.
5. Devise the platform that will gather the data and test your ideas.
6. Gather the data and see what it shows.
7. Structure the new products and services; build the supporting infrastructure and devise the new interactions that they allow.
8. Show the transformational power at the institutional and individual level and create new trust.

9. Demonstrate the new value for both parties.
10. Initiate more and more ambitious projects based on your track record together.

In this chapter, we will use the partnership between Deutsche Post-DHL and Volvo Trucks as an illustration of this sixth and last phase of the relationship-building process. Deutsche Post-DHL is a logistics company, the result of the merger of the state-owned German Post Office (the Deutsche Post component) and of the express freight integrator DHL.[1] In 2001, the two companies came together in the bold merger of two principal entities, one featuring a traditional European public service company culture, the other the result of the fast growth of a private sector company. The company made further acquisitions in the area of freight forwarding and contract logistics in the ensuing years. Today, Deutsche Post-DHL has four divisions of roughly equal size (around 12–15 billion euros each in 2014, with total revenues of about $56 billion euros): the first is the postal service, e-commerce and parcel division built largely around Deutsche Post; the second is an express freight division built around the old DHL company (it provides what is known as TDI services, where TDI stands for time-definite-international); the third is a freight forwarding division that organizes transportation logistics by airplanes, rail, road or sea; and finally, the fourth division is the one that will interest us most directly: the Supply Chain Division. Among many other customers, the Supply Chain Division delivers spare parts to the dealers of Volvo Trucks as needed.

Although most people still think of Volvo as a car company, the original Volvo company no longer makes passenger cars, having divested its passenger division in 1999 (Volvo cars are now made by the Chinese Geely group). Today, Volvo is dominated by its truck division (sales of about $22 billion), with three additional smaller divisions (construction, buses, and marine and industrial engines), bringing the company to total sales of $33 billion in 2014.[2]

DHL and Volvo Trucks have a thirty-year long history of collaboration, built on two streams of business which are managed completely independently from each other:

[1] See DHL Deutsche Post 2014 Annual Report, available at http://www.dpdhl.com/content/dam/dpdhl/Investors/Events/Reporting/2015/ar14/DPDHL_2014_Annual_Report.pdf.
[2] See Volvo Trucks 2014 Annual Report, available at http://www3.volvo.com/investors/finrep/ar14/ar_2014_eng.pdf.

- DHL buys a large number of Volvo trucks (as well as other competing trucks) for its own logistics business.
- Volvo purchases a large number of logistical services from DHL (as well as other suppliers) to deliver parts to its dealers and plants all over the world.

There is a SAM at DHL who takes care of all aspects of the commercial relationship with Volvo Trucks and routinely works with a senior buyer at Volvo; and Volvo Trucks has a SAM that takes care of all global aspects of the relationship with DHL and deals with a senior buyer at DHL. All contracts are deliberately kept separate, both for regulatory reasons, and in order to guarantee that both suppliers remain "best-of-breed" in their respective business.

This chapter exemplifies a case of how a new, initially small contract opportunity can arise from the trust that has been created between the two companies through their long-standing relationship. This new project is known as Maintenance on Demand, abbreviated as MoDe.[3] It involves the development of a high-tech data platform that allows Volvo Trucks to remain available for business 100% of the time; what is known in the trade as "uptime" or "zero downtime", and is enabled by the combination of Volvo Trucks' intrinsically high quality of products and the highly effective delivery of parts to Volvo dealers by DHL. In this chapter, we will focus on the roll-out of the MoDe project between 2012 and 2015, as an illustration of how two partners can fundamentally change their business model through work orchestrated by the SAM at the supplier firm (in our case DHL) and the senior buyer at the customer (in our case Volvo).

Here is how the ten phases of the co-creation cycle played out for Deutsche Post-DHL and Volvo Trucks on this project.

1   Identify New Problems Whose Resolution Will Change the Business Model of Both Firms Through Significant Investment

By the time you reach stage six in the relationship-building process, the two companies will have had some documented history of joint success. A culture of collaboration will have developed, allowing the two parties to discuss more freely where they want to go, therefore providing opportunities for new innovative interactions between them. This allows the SAM and the senior

---

[3] A good description of the basic MoDe concept and technology is available through a short video available at https://vimeo.com/45910498.

buyer to propose more ambitious projects they can develop together, having earned the right to such ambitions. Projects arising in this advanced stage of the relationship-building process typically tackle problems of larger scope, often of societal significance, and they require more significant investment, and are, therefore, riskier. They also require the involvement of a larger set of partners beyond the core supplier and customer, compounding the organizational complexity of the project.

In 2012, the Advanced Technology Research group of Volvo (ATR) was trying to understand what the future of truck transportation would entail. The group was looking at major societal trends, such as climate change and the need to reduce truck emissions to preserve the environment; it was also investigating the implications for its business of growing urbanization around the world (and particularly in emerging countries) and reflecting on how to improve safety for both truck drivers and the people around them. The ATR group wanted to take a lifecycle view of the problem and aimed to address these issues for the new generation of trucks at the conception stage, but also through the utilization of the trucks on the roads of the world and the eventual disposal of these vehicles.

Volvo had a twenty year-long experience of collecting truck data, using a system called Dynafleet.[4] This system is roughly comparable to the John Deere JD Link example described in Chap. 1. The firm already monitored four components of truck health: clutch, brake, battery and air drier data. It also monitored road conditions, ambient temperature, nature and weight of load and oil temperature on the truck. Many trucks had safety systems that recorded information about the driver, his state of fatigue or his behavior. While quite valuable, this information had the disadvantage of being static and "after the fact". It did not say anything about what to do at the very moment the information was recorded. It did not say "this driver should rest now", nor did it suggest "replace the front left tire now." As one commentator once cynically remarked about historical data, "all it does is help you bury the dead and shoot the wounded."

Volvo Trucks knew that connecting the information about multiple trucks in real-time to some kind of central "brain" would allow for acting proactively rather than reactively. Meanwhile, the new cloud technology and modern

---

[4] For a description of Dynafleet, see Youtube video available at https://www.youtube.com/watch?v=tQsAjU60Ens.

analytic models could do exactly that, by combining hardware, software and telecommunication modules, creating what they nicknamed an "Internet of Trucking Things" approach. This required developing new sensors, a telematics gateway, i.e., some means of sending the data to the cloud, and multiple algorithms and applications to make sense of the data and drive recommendations. Volvo Trucks developed the vision that zero unplanned stops ought to be the goal. They now had a problem formulation.

Deutsche Post-DHL was similarly pondering the future of its own industry: logistics. The Group taking on that mission is called Customer Solutions and Innovations (CSI), a name which testifies to the group's view that innovation comes from working in real time with customers rather than from some ivory tower central research lab.[5] CSI is an organization dedicated to serving 100 of the largest customers of Deutsche Post-DHL, and combines deep strategic account management capabilities (the SAMs) with innovation resources (the strategy and innovation people who work with them). This form of organization is an innovation in itself. Few companies in the world today have assembled these two capabilities in a common department, although there is an undeniable trend toward sales and R&D teaming up together to allow innovation to occur in a "live with customers" fashion. CSI was started in 2004 when all divisions decided to participate, allowing the group to become truly corporation-wide.

With Volvo Trucks, DHL could immediately see there was a unique match. The two companies knew each other well, since they were each other's customers. Both companies dealt with mobility issues. Both were interested in sustainability. The two groups had similar values. They had a series of ongoing structured interactions, such as regular customer review, where they asked each other: what else should we do, particularly on the innovation front, to build on what we have developed together already? Deutsche Post-DHL knew it would have to adapt to different business models of its customers and felt Volvo Trucks should be an excellent "lead user" for some of its emerging logistics concepts. It also knew there was enough day-to-day business in the relationship that they could start looking at longer-term time horizons, and escape the tyranny of short-term return projects.

[5] As an example of recognition received by DHL's Customer Solutions and Innovations Group, see press release on DHL receiving two SAMA Excellence Awards in 2015. The article is available at http://www.dhl.com/en/press/releases/releases_2015/group/dhl_wins_two_2015_sama_excellence_awards.html.

More specifically, Deutsche Post-DHL was beginning to think that its traditional logistics infrastructure would have to evolve to adapt to new demands from its customers. The traditional distribution center structure it used was heavily relying on centralized, economies of scale-driven, large warehouses storing a very large number of parts for its customers. This was quite efficient from a cost standpoint, but made it difficult to deliver parts quickly to the place where they were needed. DHL had created a new vision of the future of logistics that might require as much as three tiers of distribution centers, a combination of global, regional and local centers geared to deliver parts very quickly to dealers who needed them. This would have a cost implication, but would dramatically reduce the lead time involved in delivering a part to its point of use. In the most ambitious form of the vision, it would even allow dealers to get rid of their own inventory, letting the dealer outsource the inventory management function to DHL. DHL found itself thinking that the connected truck and zero downtime vision of Volvo Trucks might be a good match with its own vision of local distribution centers delivering parts to dealers in quasi-real time. Now, this was an exciting problem to work on together!

2   Involve New Players Outside the Two Core Firms in Tackling the Problem You Have Identified

The more complex the problem you tackle, the more players you're likely to need to solve it. By the time you reach stage six of the relationship-building process, chances are you will need a lot more than the core supplier and customer in your ecosystem. This requires that you undertake research to figure out who can contribute in the areas neither of the two core companies can address, and that you approach them with a convincing story that motivates them to join the community of players you are assembling. This, of course, also poses governance and contractual issues we will address in the next section. SAMs and senior buyers have a key role to play in assembling the network of entities required to solve the problem. The identification of the right technical players is usually done by R&D or product management groups in the respective companies, but the initial approach and "selling" of the collaborative vision is often handled by the SAMs and senior buyers.

In our Deutsche Post-DHL and Volvo Trucks partnership for the Maintenance-on-Demand project, the European Community (EC) played a very important federating and funding role. In fact, as both parties acknowledge, "without them, the project would have never taken off".[6] In 2012, the European Community (EC) was looking to fund a project that would foster the development of an Internet of Things infrastructure in the logistics area. Although this type of government funding is sometimes viewed as wasteful by many private sector businesses, particularly in the US, the story in this chapter shows that government entities can play a useful role in setting up the collaborative framework (and the funding) for complex ecosystem projects. Volvo Trucks, as a Swedish company, and Deutsche Post-DHL, through its German heritage and Belgian headquarters, were quite aware that there was public financing available for such a project and started investigating whether it could tap into those funds. Over the ensuing three years, the EU contributed 5.7 million euros to the project, in effect de-risking the entire project for both firms.

Counting Deutsche Post-DHL and Volvo Trucks, nine partners were involved in the MoDe project.[7] Here is who they were and what they contributed:

- Deutsche Post-DHL (Belgium headquarters): defined the user requirements, using its own drivers, dispatchers and fleet engineers as "guinea pigs" for the MoDe system.
- Volvo Trucks (Sweden): developed a smart service planning tool geared to maximize uptime for the trucks.
- Continental Teves (Germany): provided the sensor technology required for the shock absorber system (called "damper" in Europe).
- Fraunhoffer ISS (Germany): developed the energy-efficient wireless communication system.
- LMS (Belgium): evaluated the effectiveness of in-vehicle sensors for condition-monitoring.
- Avonwood (UK): was responsible for the design, development and integration of the Radio Frequency Identification technology.
- University of Technology of Troyes (France): tested lifetime models for vehicle components and created algorithms to estimate remaining life of those components and decisions on when to fix them.
- VTT (Finland): worked on estimating life of a shock absorber.

[6] Interviews of Pascal Kemps, DHL; Hayder Wokil; Volvo Trucks; and Pascal Claes, Volvo Trucks, September 2015.
[7] See brochure entitled Future-Proofing the Automotive Industry, available at http://fp7-mode.eu/userfiles/downloads/MoDe.pdf.

- Mobisoft (Finland): developed a tool to identify the perfect location to do repair on trucks which had been identified as having a problem.

Drilling down to the individuals involved inside Deutsche Post-DHL and Volvo Trucks reveals an even greater organizational complexity. More than 20 core people spread over five departments were involved in the project.

On the Volvo Trucks side, the team included the following:

- The Advanced Technology Research department (ATR).
- The Commercial Sales department.
- The Market/Dealer Service department.

Both the Commercial Sales and the Market/Dealer Service departments also had to become involved, both at corporate headquarters, and at the country level.

On the Deutsche Post-DHL side, the following people were involved:

- The Customer Solutions and Innovations group (CSI)
- The Fleet team representing the operational unit

Figure 9.1 illustrates the various organizational entities (communities) that had to come together in order to to design and operationalize the various streams of value involved in the Maintenance-on-Design project. The rest of this chapter describes how the *a priori* architecture of the project envisioned by the two companies at the outset played out over time.

While the project was of daunting complexity when one considers the number of players involved at both the institutional and individual level, the participants found a way to make it work. The transformative power of the effort, the trust that had been developed from the long-standing relationship, and the de-risking of the project made possible by the European Community's funding all had a lot to do with its success.

3   Agree on an IP Sharing Structure and Governance Process that Engages the Various Sides and Protects Their Interests

To deal with the complexity of large projects involving multiple parties, you need a legal framework to define who will retain what intellectual property (IP) as a result of the collaboration, and a governance process that lays out the rules through which the group will make key decisions. Both imply a major

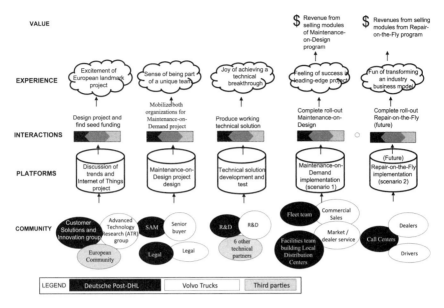

Fig. 9.1   Co-creation value map of Deutsche Post-DHL and Volvo Trucks working together on maintenance-on-demand project. This chart is also available at http://www.eccpartnership. com/the-co-creation-edge.html

role transformation for your legal department and managers, so be prepared for a bit of a rocky road as you confront these two issues.

Most legal departments are trained to jealously protect the IP of their firm, an attitude, which by definition, makes it difficult to engage in any deep collaborative endeavor. In the modern world, where B2B collaboration is increasingly mandatory, it is not uncommon for the two legal departments of supplier and customer to butt heads. Corporate legal training has, by and large, not yet caught up with the new world of co-creation, so be prepared to have to provide heavy coaching to your IP folks. In a collaborative partnership, the last thing you want is to have your IP buried so deep in your back yard that it cannot be touched by the other members of the ecosystem. This will defeat the very purpose of the collaborative effort (and sadly, some firms that are dominated by their legal department die at this stage). Yes, it is your IP department's role to make sure that the organization's IP is not inadvertently made available for free to others, but to come alive and generate value, your IP needs to be put in contact with other partners' IP, and your legal department will have to cut you some slack in framing the IP contracts for the advanced collaboration described in this chapter.

On the governance front, you will need to set up a multi-stakeholder steering committee and a joint core team to run the project. While most managers have typically received a lot of coaching in the last twenty years on the need to work in participative fashion, for example, by using 360-degree feedback and other HR techniques, none of this training has prepared managers for the introduction of extraneous bodies from other firms. Be prepared for some inevitable hiccups in the implementation of any multi-party governance structure. Depending on the degree to which your company relies on a command-and-control culture, the number of managers willing to let go of their controlling instincts may be limited; as a SAM or senior buyer, be prepared to coach, coach and coach again. Gird yourself for sarcasm on the "management by committee", meeting-itis, and initiatives overload. Keep the prize in front of people at all times.

In the MoDe project, the European Community, in addition to promoting and funding the project, also provided an IP legal structure in three tiers that acted as reference framework for Deutsche Post-DHL and Volvo Trucks. The EU IP framework defines three categories of contracts, each with its own level of confidentiality:

1. Partners can decide to only share with the EU, but not share anything with other partners.
2. Partners can decide to share their IP among partners, but not outside the group.
3. Partners can decide to make everything public.

Understandably, you cannot do a funded EU project where the partners keep everything private.

In the end, the partners ended up working with a fairly loose series of individual agreements:

• Every company agreed to keep its IP.
• There was no formal co-development contract, and self-interest of the individual parties drove the work in natural fashion.
• Deutsche Post-DHL agreed with the EU that it would make public the new logistics service it developed as a result of MoDe (e.g., distribution center structure), but did not have to share the process through which it

was going to manage the new network of distribution centers, making it difficult for competitors to copy its model.

On the governance front, both companies set up a joint Steering Committee that met formally every six months during the project, supplemented by monthly meetings and conference calls and numerous technical meetings by the parties involved in each work stream. There again, the fact that the two core companies had worked together for years, and trusted each other, obviated the need for tightly defined legal contracts.

4   Formulate Specific Hypotheses on Where the Business Value Will Lie in the New Mode of Interaction

Although it is not always possible to pinpoint the exact benefits that will accrue from the new innovative capability being developed, the SAM and senior buyer should attempt to formulate the business case for the investment as early, and in as crispy a fashion as possible. Technologists like to speak about "use case", or occasionally "scenario", which are essentially a visualization of how the technology will be used in the field, often without the return-on-investment component. At the minimum, SAM and senior buyer, working with the technical people, should develop the logic of that business case, if not necessarily the magnitude of it (precise return-on-investment calculations on large, infrastructure projects are often illusory).

As indicated in earlier chapters, the modeling of future business value should comprise a mix of deterministic logic (e.g., "we believe that if we measure wear and tear on a tire through a sensor, this will reduce the amount of unscheduled downtime for the driver, because we will, for example, be able to change the tire before it develops a problem") and data-driven exploration (e.g., we are not sure whether measuring the amount of vibration in the cabin is indicative of anything, but since the cost of collecting that data is not very high, let's collect it and find out heuristically later on if it correlates with anything").

For the MoDe project, Deutsche Post-DHL and Volvo Trucks visualized a simple *before* and *after* mode of operation:

Before MoDe:

- Unpredicted wear and tear goes undetected between maintenance checks.

- Eventual damage is more unpredictable, extensive and costly.
- Breakdowns and accidents can occur.
- Time waiting for assistance, sourcing parts and dealing with emergencies expands.
- Vehicle downtime grows.
- Customer dissatisfaction increases.

After MoDe, the system provides four primary benefits:

1. It produces safer travel:

    Chances of breakdowns and accidents are radically reduced by early fault detection. This avoids associated congestion.

2. It is more economical:

    With fewer and shorter breakdowns and unplanned stops, vehicle uptime is boosted by 30%. More accurate and timely feedback means more efficient repairs and less risk of human errors.

3. The company remains in complete control:

    The system's centralized synchronization makes possible remote monitoring, vehicle reconfiguration and ongoing analysis for better decision-making.

4. It allows environmental gains:

    By making sure vehicles are serviced at exactly the right time, sub-optimal performance is reduced. Unnecessary part replacements are avoided and driving time to maintenance locations are cut down. Fuel consumption is optimized and carbon dioxide emissions cut.

They now had a good picture of where the benefits would accrue and had identified the metrics they should track during implementation. The next task was to build the actual platform.

5   Devise the Platform that Will Gather the Data and Test Your Ideas

The technical development of a data platform in an advanced stage of supplier-customer relationship is a complex affair. Neither the SAM, nor the senior buyer are expected to lead the development process, but they often play a key role in facilitating it through the access they have inside the partner firm. The definition of user requirements, for example, can greatly benefit from the SAM, or the senior buyer directing the technical team to influential people who play a vocal role inside the partner firm. They can expedite the process when people do not make themselves available promptly enough. Most importantly, they can keep the development process moving and communicate early successes to sustain the momentum.

In the MoDe project, as is generally the case for Internet of Things project, the technology "stack" that needed to be assembled was particularly complex. It included six major streams of development[8]:

- First, the technical team had to develop new sensors able to capture real-time data from the truck in four areas: engine, injector system, oil system and shock absorber system.
- It also needed to develop a central unit in the cab that could aggregate this data and process its information.
- It then needed to be able to send this information to the cloud through a telecommunication gateway, allowing the data to be combined with other data and analyzed for meaning.
- It then needed to have a suite of algorithms and applications that could make sense of that information and suggest what maintenance decisions should be made in light of the data.
- Eventually, Volvo Trucks had to develop preventive repair processes that responded intelligently to the new information.
- As the Volvo Truck supplier-partner, Deutsche Post-DHL had to develop new infrastructure and parts delivery processes to serve the new preventive maintenance process devised by Volvo Trucks.

The project could have failed at each of these stages, but it did not.

6   Gather the Data and See What You Have

The purpose of the platform development proof-of-concept phase is to check whether both companies (and their partners) have generated something they can use, or not. Success requires that two outcomes be present. First, the technology has to work, e.g., the sensors must technically be able to capture

---

[8] For a conceptual description of what constitutes an Internet of Things ecosystem, see article written by Michael Porter and James Heppelman, entitled *How Smart, Connected Products are Transforming Competition*, Harvard Business Review, November 2014.

the necessary data, and the gateway to the cloud needs to be able to send the data to the network and its servers. But second, the data needs to produce insights that can be used to produce valuable business results for both companies and their partners.

The role of the SAM and the senior buyer is to be the interpreter of those early technical results. If successful, their role becomes one of advocate for those results. While the technology issues can be nerdy or geeky, the role of the SAM and the senior buyer is to act as a secular interpreter of the early successes of the proof-of-concept phase and to start preparing the ground for the eventual commercialization of products and services that will ensue.

There was a lot of trial and error in this phase of the MoDe project. One of the key components of the experiment was to prove that the sensors could "see" problems developing more effectively than trained drivers. To test that, Volvo Trucks and its technology partners mounted a series of sensors on trucks and let professional drivers drive them around. They then changed some subtle parameters, for example replacing a regular shock absorber with a slightly damaged one to see whether the professional driver noticed. He did not, but the sensor did. They did the same with the antenna aimed at identifying other vehicles coming within a dangerous perimeter of the truck. The professional driver did not notice it, but the antenna did. The same was true for subtle changes in energy consumption. In all of these cases, the "machine" beat the human perception of even highly trained drivers. The technology worked!

On another front, the data experts at the University of Troyes wowed the group by showing they could indeed come up with good estimates of a part's remaining life, given data on how the part had been used. The math was esoteric, but the model worked. This was all the group wanted to know.

For predictive model-building, the challenge proved one of simplification. Because the new sensors capture lots of new data that was then added on top of the data Volvo Trucks was already collecting, the problem became one of sifting through the morass and identifying the few items that really matter for preventive maintenance purposes. Data experts, like doctors, can build richly textured diagnostics for each truck situation and their expertise will indeed produce extraordinarily refined prescriptions for action. But Volvo Trucks could hardly afford to have an exquisite diagnostician looking at each truck individually. All it needed was a "good enough" prescription for all the trucks at all times, using a computer-operated algorithm.

They passed the test. The sensors worked. They could estimate the remaining life of the various parts fairly accurately. They could devise smart algorithms and applications that produced good recommendations. They had proven at the conceptual stage that they could reduce unplanned downtime. They were off to the races.

7   Structure the New Products and Services, Build the Supporting Infrastructure, and Devise the New Interactions that They Allow

Once the technical feasibility of the project has been proven, the two companies has to structure the products and services they want to market or source, and start selling them. Most companies have product management functions playing this role, but SAMs and senior buyers should work closely with them to vet the practical feasibility of the packaged products and services they envision. Once this is done, the more traditional part of the role of the SAM and the senior buyer kicks in.

Both companies will likely have to build new infrastructure to support the use of the new platform and delivery of the new products and services. In some cases, this may represent considerable effort. They will also have to devise new processes and interactions between them, including a new way to negotiate with each other.

On the products and services front, Deutsche Post-DHL and Volvo Trucks have created 11 "work packages" that they sell individually to third parties in the automotive aftermarkets, for example, to the numerous commercial fleets that utilize Volvo Trucks. Each work package involves a set of defined products, or services, to which a price has been assigned. From there on, the role of the SAMs and senior buyers becomes a more traditional one, i.e., they sell or source a defined set of benefits generated by these work packages.

On the infrastructure side, Volvo Trucks had a lot of the needed infrastructure already in place, such as back-office IT and call centers. Deutsche Post-DHL, though, had to develop a new warehouse architecture that utilizes a three-tiered structure where there had previously been only two:

- Traditionally, the passenger and commercial vehicle industry operates big Global Distribution Centers (GDCs) or Central Distribution Centers (CDCs). These are a first storage location fed by the component suppliers, start at 700,000 square feet, and operate as standalone facility. Its geographical range is global or super-regional. It handles upwards of 60,000 stock keeping units (SKUs) and stocks all parts for all car or truck model types.

- The second-tier structure is called Parts Distribution centers (PDC) and are fed by the Global Distribution Center. Their role is to deliver to dealers of the car or truck company (such as Volvo Trucks). These are also known as Regional Distribution Centers (RDC's), or sometimes National Distribution Centers (or NDC's) by the car or truck companies. Their geographical range is typically national; they start at around 150,000 square feet, and also operate as standalone facilities. They typically handle upwards of 40,000 SKUs and cater to all parts for car or truck types sold in the area.

- The newcomer in the Deutsche Post-DHL architecture is a developing concept called the Local Distribution Center or LDC. It is fed by a Parts Distribution Center (or more and more often by the GDC/CDC) and delivers to dealers. Its geographical range is up to 130 miles from dealers; its area starts at around 10,000 square feet, and it is a shared user facility. It has upward of 5,000 SKUs, and is focused on fast-moving parts for area car and truck types. These LDCs are typically clustered in a network and enable same day delivery of parts. They are the missing link that allows manufacturers to complete a repair, even if it is an unplanned repair.

The negotiation process has also dramatically changed since a lot of new value has now been created at the intersection of both firms. Deutsche Post-DHL is no longer playing in a commodity game dominated by a price-focused procurement process that neutralizes any differentiation between suppliers. It can point to the high level of parts availability the firm provides, and dense service networks that allow customers to not have to drive far for service. Selling these benefits effectively requires that the DHL SAM be in the procurement cycle early and place himself in a position to work with the fleet people rather than be kept away from them.

8   Build the Individual and Institutional Trust by Winning Together

In stage six of the relationship-building process, you should aim to transform the individual experience of all major players in the ecosystem at both a rational and emotional level. If you, as a SAM or senior buyer, can orchestrate such a movement on a large scale, you will unleash a collective transformation that will ultimately create its own dynamics and become unstoppable. This should be your goal in stage six of the relationship-building process.

The first part of a transformational experience involves bringing a rational solution to the other party's problem, by creating an objectively measurable outcome (say, helping your counterpart produce better numbers) that she can use to show her superiors that she is doing a good job. This objective improvement will engender a flow of empathy from your counterpart, and she is likely to want to reciprocate and help you, which will trigger a counter-flow of empathy on your part. By encouraging this scenario to repeat itself across multiple parties in both organizations, SAMs and senior buyers have the power to drive major cross-company transformations.

If you succeed, you will engender a new institutional trust between the companies involved. What is often characterized by pundits as "a new collaborative culture" or "trust" is never legislated from on high by top managers of both firms (although top-level collaboration helps!). It is always the result of a series of successful bottom-up joint initiatives where individuals learn to work together long enough to achieve joint success. It is the collective aggregation of these small pockets of success turning into streams of empathy that we ultimately call "trust" or "collaborative culture". In other words, trust and collaborative cultures are the result of a large number of small empathy flows encouraged by the SAM and the senior buyer.

With MoDe, it is easy to visualize the rational and emotional wins for most players in the new system. Truck drivers feel more secure and know the system is watching over their truck. One of the golden rules of the MoDe development was that the driver should barely know the system is there. For example, there is no additional screen to look at, and no expectation of additional work for drivers—less hassle, more reliability of the truck and safety for the driver.

Volvo Trucks dealers no longer have to manage a large inventory, often full of obsolete parts (it is not uncommon for dealers to carry inventories of $100,000 or more, plus they incur the associated cost of the land which can be quite high around big cities). They don't have to sweat the parts availability issue anymore, reversing the old curse of the truck business: "if you don't have the part, you don't have the service." They are happy because they improve their bottom-line, remove their inventory risk and stop losing sleep over lost sales.

For the Volvo Trucks and Deutsche Post-DHL team members involved, one can also identify the transformational nature of the project they have done together: growth in sales from Deutsche Post-DHL to Volvo Trucks and growth from Volvo Trucks to Deutsche Post-DHL have clearly benefitted the two SAMs, for example.

But beyond the sheer numbers, members of the two firms describe the new bond between the two firms in surprisingly affective fashion.[9] "We like each other" says one interviewee. "We work comfortably with each other." "Our relationship is friendly and noncompetitive, almost nonbusiness-like." Says another interviewee, "You don't have to talk about today's problem; we don't discuss cost and budget every day. Here, we're thinking long-term; we think in very open-minded ways. This is directly linked to all that openness." Another interviewee puts it this way, "We (both DHL and Volvo Trucks) still run our Requests for Quotes in exactly the same way as we did before, but when we talk, value is mutually validated. Or if it isn't validated yet, there is a proven track record that commitments and statements are accurate and will be lived up to. Those are tangible, measurable decision criteria in a procurement process."

At this stage, hardcore readers may be skeptical of this soft collaborative language, or dismissive of its role in a business story, but it is hard to deny that those two companies have accomplished something quite unique in their relationship.

9   Let the New Value Model Emerge for Both Parties

When you reach stage six of the relationship-building model, the value model you will have to build is typically more "big picture" and discovery-oriented, and less prescriptive and analytical. Instead of justifying the project on a deterministic sequence of causes and effects ("if we do this, the following will happen"), partner companies often sketch out a big vision for the future business model for both parties (or more), but do not attempt to map out, or quantify, every analytical detail in the flow of future revenues, cost, investment and risk.

This may sound surprising to SAMs and senior buyers who are used to justifying every resource-requiring initiative on the basis of some economic return or business case, often under the scrutiny of a project management office supervised by a financial person. While some companies are intrinsically more hard-nosed than others on the business case requirement (American

[9] Interviews of Pascal Kemps, DHL; Hayder Wokil; Volvo Trucks; and Pascal Claes, Volvo Trucks, September 2015.

companies often remark that their European competitors have more latitude in that regard), we have repeatedly found that companies that have achieved good operational results together for many years relax some of those short-term, analytically-based requirements for cooperative projects, and let themselves wander into less chartered territories, having developed enough goodwill to take greater risks together. One can argue that this ability to explore new models together is the single largest source of competitive advantage for both firms, further reinforcing why the SAM and the senior buyer should try to take their respective company to this advanced stage of co-creation.

Often, companies find it useful to agree on a conceptualization of value "scenario", or "waves of value" they envision. Others refer to this as a "stairway of value" (sometimes also called "stairway to heaven", perhaps in homage to the rock group Led Zeppelin) that represents various planks of value the two companies reach over time.

Deutsche Post-DHL and Volvo Trucks are a good illustration of the simultaneous transformation of both companies' business model. Since value is a function of revenues, cost, investment and risk, we need to acknowledge that the project was tremendously helped on the risk front by the generous technology investment made by the European Community into the project (few projects receive a €5.8 million endowment at the beginning!). Beyond the technology investment made (mostly) with third-parties, though, Volvo Trucks and Deutsche Post-DHL still had to make a significant investment in time and salary for their own people, and did so on each company's nickel. Volvo Trucks did most of the work at the beginning, and Deutsche Post-DHL's investment grew steadily as the distribution center structure required to support the new Volvo Trucks model began to emerge.

To describe how value was going to accrue to both companies, Deutsche Post-DHL and Volvo Trucks have constructed two value scenarios, one which has largely been implemented today, and the second that is only now materializing.[10] Scenario 1 is entitled *Maintenance on Demand* and assumes that trucks are still serviced at traditional truck dealers, while Scenario 2, called *Repair-on-the-Fly*, envisions that trucks will eventually be serviced by mobile workshops by the side of the road.

Here is how the companies describe each scenario.

---

[10] See brochure entitled Future-Proofing the Automotive Industry, available at http://fp7-mode.eu/userfiles/downloads/MoDe.pdf.

Scenario 1: Maintenance-on-Demand

Now: the vehicle maintenance contracts sold with a vehicle rely on "static" information provided at the time of a sale.

The MoDe vision: Services are tailored to a vehicle's exact configuration, mission, and the dynamic feedback of information. Reducing periods of vehicle unavailability means that businesses can better achieve their objectives.

In practice: Dealers and their clients agree what is required by the business up front. Uptime needs, the exact configuration of the vehicle, and service needs are then considered within the sales process. This level of tailoring makes it easier to precisely plan vehicle stops, and makes service provision far more dynamic.

Scenario 2: Repair-on-the-Fly

Now: Drivers are warned of problems by an on-board system. They then report the issue to a call center. But the location of the vehicle and the nature of the problem aren't always obvious, making it difficult to get the right parts delivered to the right place at the right time.

The MoDe vision: Roadside repairs are made more efficient. Condition monitoring and estimates of remaining lifetime help detect failures in advance. Key information is communicated to a central system, which calculates the nearest and most suitable workshop for the repairs.

In practice: Where it is not possible to reach a workshop, the MoDe system will advise drivers of the "best location to stop". Details will be sent to mobile workshops equipped with the resources needed to make roadside repairs, and the vehicle will be met at an agreed "meeting point". An efficient spare parts management system will be set up to support this process.

Today, the Maintenance-on-Demand scenario is being implemented for all new trucks. The Maintenance-on-the-Fly scenario constitutes an aspiration and a model for the future.

10   *Initiate More and More Projects Based on Your Track Record Together*

Co-creation is an ever-expanding universe. The more success the SAM and the senior buyer experience through their collaboration, the more new opportunities will emerge involving new problems, new individuals or organizational entities, additional partners, new platform ideas, or other value-creating schemes. Since opportunities occur by fostering new points of interactions between the companies, the greater the number of existing interactions, the more likely it is that the two parties will find additional ways to connect with each other, making the growth between the two firms exponential. Otherwise stated, the larger the existing cooperative system between the two firms, the more it is likely to grow further into the future. The role of the SAM and the senior buyer involves continuously growing the collaborative network and keeping it active.

In this chapter, we focused on the Maintenance-on-Demand project to illustrate how a sweeping transformational project emerged from a long-standing operationally-based relationship between the two firms. But the two firms have many other projects in the works, such as jointly designing a new hybrid diesel-electric truck model, or developing a roadside maintenance model together. In a recent presentation, the DHL-Volvo Trucks offered this encouragement to other companies interested in this advanced form of platform-based co-innovation: "Getting started is much easier than you think."

This chapter marks the end of our description of the six phases of the relationship-building model. We now turn to our final chapter and suggest how the co-creative process results in five layers of competitive advantage as the relationship between supplier and customer grows.

CHAPTER 10

The Five Levels of Competitive Advantage Yielded by Co-Creation for Sales and Procurement

In the final chapter, we summarize what can be achieved by going through the co-creative relationship-building process we have described in this book. Rather than focus on the process of co-creation as we have done so far, we now review what outcomes or results you should target for your co-creation program. The logic of the process is the same: no matter how ambitious your co-creation program is, the scope of your program will change as a function of how you define the problem, how many people you are prepared to involve in your problem-solving community, how much data you want to look at and how innovative the value model is you are trying to create.

We have found that suppliers and customers using co-creation can aim for *five levels of competitive advantage*, from targeting a limited operational change agenda all the way to pursuing a sweeping strategic or transformative ambition. See Fig. 10.1.

In order of increasing difficulty, you may strive for any or all of the following five goals:

1. Redefine the relationship between sales and procurement.
2. Improve the customer and supplier operations.
3. Introduce and develop new products together.
4. Redesign the value chain by involving customers' customers and suppliers' suppliers.
5. Transform an entire ecosystem's business model.

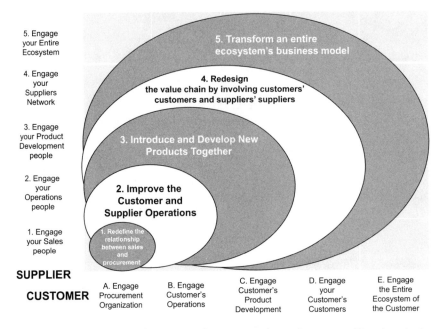

Fig. 10.1 The five levels of co-creation between supplier and customer. This chart is also available at http://www.eccpartnership.com/the-co-creation-edge.html

These five degrees of competitive advantage generally correlate with the six steps of the relationship-building process described in the preceding five chapters. There is a stairway-like quality, and, therefore, natural order to these five levels: generally, the best way to reach the higher level transformative levels is to first implement the lower-level transformation. In some cases, companies have been able to leap-frog directly to the upper transformative levels, but this is a difficult and risky path.

For each of our five levels of competitive advantage, we identify where each case study described earlier in the book fits with a particular level of competitive advantage. For the more advanced forms of competitive advantage (levels three, four and five), we also introduce new examples showing how real-life SAMs and senior buyers went about producing these levels of competitive advantage for their firms. (Because the modeling of community-building, data analysis or value generation gets more complex for those advanced forms of co-creation, they do not lend themselves to the simpler "pedagogical" exposition of the process in the earlier chapters).

1　Level One: Redefine the Relationship Between Sales and Procurement

The first level of co-creation involves *redefining the relationship between sales and procurement*. The sales-procurement interaction is generally viewed as transactional, but it can be a source of innovation when both sales and procurement organizations engage differently with each other. The sales and procurement processes that can be made co-creative include the creation of specifications for products and services by the customer, the development of proposals by the supplier, and the pricing process contained in those proposals.

The Hotel Co-RoadWarriors case introduced in Chap. 5 is an example of this approach. Not every industry has a ready-made platform to do dynamic pricing. As we saw with the Hotel Co-RoadWarriors case, though, the hotel industry does, as do airlines and other public transportation systems. For manufacturing industries and B2B services, the dynamic sales and procurement platforms often have to be developed, but the same potential exists. Most B2B industries could implement the same productivity gains through a co-creative approach between sales and procurement.

Co-creation can solve many problems. Many RFPs involve too much process and not enough content. The number of suppliers being consulted is often too high, producing perfunctory responses by suppliers who do not trust that they are actually being considered for real business. Many suppliers fail to standardize, or modularize, their proposal format, leading to constant reinvention of the wheel. Customers also often over-design their RFPs rather than trust suppliers to frame the RFP. All of this is attributable to the fact that customers are viewed as passive recipients of a process driven by suppliers, rather than the two of them acting as transaction co-creators.

There is some good news on the horizon, though. After many years of seeing the brute force mode of negotiation dominate the market, we are seeing growing interest on the part of procurement departments in engaging suppliers in co-creation, such as in the automotive sector, a traditional bastion of ruthless price negotiation. Ultimately, we predict that we will see the emergence of other sales-procurement co-creation platforms beyond the dynamic pricing platform that has been the main focus so far in this area.

2   *Level Two: Improve the Customer's and Supplier's Operations*

A second, deeper level of co-creation is to *improve the customer's and supplier's operations* simultaneously. This form of competitive advantage is the one most frequently pursued by companies that engage in co-creation. This is done by having the supplier set up a platform that monitors the customer's operations, then having the supplier generate insights with the customer on how to run their operations more effectively. Eventually, the value of the data generated at the customer level causes the supplier to modify his operations to provide continuously more valuable insights to the customer.

The improvement can involve a rise in quality or yield in a manufacturing environment, a reduction in cost or capital expenditures in the delivery of a service, or greater effectiveness in after-sales service in the field for a product or service. The new link being created requires building a new connection between supplier and customer, but also developing connections between some of the previously unconnected groups inside the customer. Some platforms are built into the product itself (for example, most cars have several digital systems built in them like GPS sensors or diagnostics), while others have to be built separately from the product or service provided.

The Ecolab case used in Chap. 2 is an example of this level of ambition, as is the Xerox Managed Print Services introduced in Chap. 6. In this second level of co-creation, the role of the sales person is initially to work with her procurement counterpart and facilitate the development and adoption of the proposed platform within their respective organizations. Once the engagement process is established, they orchestrate the development and piloting of the platform. When the platform is in place, they foster its use by the relevant operating departments to produce the desired results.

John Deere Construction whom we mentioned briefly as a vignette in Chap. 1, is another example of a company that improves its construction company customers' operations. In 2014, Deere's Construction Division sold $6.6 billion worth of equipment through 600 global dealers, making it second in the market behind Caterpillar (John Deere is best known for its agriculture equipment where it is the global leader).[1] Construction equipment dealers are

---

[1] For a basic description of John Deere Construction and Forestry division, see https://www.deere.com/en_US/industry/construction/john_deere_construction_forestry_division/john_deere_construction_and_forestry_division.page.

the first-order customers managed by the SAMs of Deere Construction, and the construction companies are Deere's indirect customers.

For construction companies (and their dealer suppliers), the main issue is to deliver a construction project on-time and on budget. This requires minimizing operating cost and capital expenditures on every site, both of which are heavily dependent on the effective use of the construction machines. To generate insights for the construction company, John Deere has developed the John Deere WorkSight® platform[2] that records data about how each machine is used, generating field data that allows these individuals to solve problems together as a team.

The platform improves operations in many ways. First, it helps reduce energy consumption by tracking how every machine is used onsite. For example, foremen can see which operators let the machine idle for hours when its engine should be turned off, allowing some coaching. By monitoring machine utilization, construction managers can see whether they have too few or too many machines for the job at hand, which optimizes their capital expenditures for the site. John Deere WorkSight® also has sensors that capture whether operators are wearing down the equipment through their operating style, e.g., if they attack hard rocks with too much vigor, thereby prematurely wearing out some of the mechanical parts. The platform also allows the construction manager to draw a virtual perimeter around each machine, which allows WorkSight® to send a signal if the machine leaves this perimeter, which prevents machine theft on the site, or unauthorized use of a machine.

There is both an emotional benefit and a bottom-line value to the system. Emotionally, WorkSight® makes everybody's job easier, because of the availability of data and the problem-solving structure offered by Deere. On the value side, the system produces a triple financial win for the construction company customer (reduced operating and capital costs), the dealer (more sales) and Deere Construction (also more sales).

The role of the Deere sales person is to engage his procurement counterpart in seeing how much value can be created together through the John Deere WorkSight® capabilities. The procurement person's role at the construction company, in addition to her traditional price negotiation role, is to encourage

---

[2] In January 2015, John Deere Construction released a series of videos that explain how the Worksight™ system works. They are available at: https://www.deere.com/en_US/corporate/our_company/news_and_media/press_releases/2015/construction/2015jan14-worksight.page.

operating people in the company to use the data generated and capture the operational benefits made possible by the Deere technology. Psychologically, this demands that the buyer acquire new operational skills which may come in handy for career progression.

Of course, neither the strategic account manager, nor the procurement manager at the construction company are single-handedly doing all this connecting of people and generating of new data and insights. Their role is to orchestrate the process through which all parties at Deere, its dealers and its customers come together to generate those new performance insights.

The improvement of operations at John Deere's construction companies, which we characterize as level two co-creation in our nomenclature, also induces some other effects. Sales and procurement people now have another basis for their contract negotiation with the savings created on construction sites, and they no longer have to beat each other up on price, which allows for a change in the nature of the sales and procurement process (level one co-creation in this chapter's nomenclature). Also the existence of a steady data feed of information back to Deere on how the machines are actually used on construction sites allows Deere engineers to continuously learn how the machines behave in the field, allowing them to incorporate new features in the next generation of machines (which we will describe as level three co-creation in the next section).

3 Level Three: Introduce and Develop New Products Together

The third level of co-creative competitive advantage for sales and procurement involves ushering into the process the Research and Development (R&D) departments on both sides. This is a less frequent form of co-creation than the level three, operations-driven co-creation today, but it is arguably the fastest growing form of co-creation pursuit. This often starts with the supplier's R&D department engaging with the customer to solve a technical problem, as we saw with the Techelec case in Chap. 3. Over time, the supplier's R&D department develops the credibility to engage the customer's R&D department. This particular form of co-creation is sometimes called *co-innovation*.

There again, sales and procurement people have a key role to play. Technical people rarely have the wherewithal to do the relationship-building and project management work required to sustain those efforts. Many of them prefer working at their laboratory than become global road warriors. The best sales people learn to partner with R&D people, giving them the opportunity to shine while protecting them from the vicissitudes of the selling cycle. Procurement people must learn to play a similar role by engaging their firm's R&D people, thereby providing an answer to the challenge often uttered by their management to push their suppliers to be more innovative.

The German specialty chemical company Altana[3] and its customer, BASF Coatings, a division of the largest chemical company in the world, also headquartered in Germany[4] offer an example of how R&D departments can co-create products when orchestrated by enlightened sales and procurement people on both sides. In 2014, Altana's revenues reached €1.95 billion in revenues, with an honorable Return on Capital Employed of 10.3%.[5] The company is made up of four major divisions and 50 operating companies, and has grown substantially through 30 acquisitions made over the last ten years.

One of Altana's original strategic challenges was to bring together the full power of all its operating entities for customers like BASF Coatings. BASF Coatings had revenues of €3.9 billion in 2014, and is part of the larger BASF empire (2014 sales of €74.3 billion).[6]

A few years back, Altana initiated a strategic account management program where a single sales person has responsibility for bringing together all the capabilities of the firm for the customer. One of the most striking accomplishments of the partnership Altana established between its account management and R&D functions is the joint "cockpit" the firm has built with BASF Coatings.[7] The cockpit is a true technical co-creation platform that is developed and used by a cross-company team consisting of representatives from BASF, and the BASF account management team, and technical resources of the BYK and Eckart divisions of Altana.

---

[3] See company website for general introduction to the company (http://www.altana.com/).

[4] See BASF Coatings website at http://www.basf-coatings.com/global/ecweb/en/.

[5] Source: Altana 2014 Annual Report, available at http://www.altana.com/company/annual-report.html.

[6] See BASF 2014 Annual Report, available at https://www.basf.com/documents/corp/en/about-us/publications/reports/2015/BASF_Report_2014.pdf.

[7] See page 16-21 in 2012 Altana Annual Report for a description of the cockpit approach. The report is available at http://www.altana.com/fileadmin/altana/press_news/publications/GB_2012_ALTANA_e.pdf.

The greatest value generated by the Altana-BASF cockpit platform comes from the sharing of each company's technical road map, the joint collection of operational data, and the development of joint hypotheses on how to optimize the integrated supply chain, all the way to the application of the coatings on the car (and sometimes beyond to the servicing of the car and its end of life, when automotive manufacturers are willing to share that data).

The joint development done in the Altana-BASF cockpit also produces a ripple effect back to Altana's own manufacturing (level two co-creation in our model). For example, BASF Coatings helped Altana develop a new quality measurement process that has now been implemented at the main plant of Altana's BYK division in Wesel. As a result of the cockpit, the role of the account manager at Altana and the procurement person responsible for Altana, has changed dramatically (level one co-creation). There is still a hard price negotiation process between the two firms, but the dialogue is now driven by the agenda set by the cockpit.

Altana and BASF Coatings are a strong example of R&D co-creation, or co-innovation. While not many companies develop the trust required to make a joint investment of this magnitude, there is evidence of a strong trend toward co-located R&D and increased risk-sharing between customer and supplier. Product developers are slowly learning to engage in co-creation, with sales and procurement people providing them with the framework to do it.

4 Level Four: Redesign the Value Chain by Involving Customers' Customers and Suppliers' Suppliers

The fourth level of co-creation involves engaging the customer's customer and the supplier's suppliers. While it would appear logical for a supplier to extend the co-creation process to its own suppliers and a customer to their own customers, procurement and sales groups rarely meet inside a typical corporation. This is arguably one of the most broken links in the co-creative chain. Many sales people bemoaning the difficulty of engaging their customers' procurement departments into innovative activity do not realize that their own procurement group is often one of the worst offenders. Similarly, many procurement departments do not understand that their unwillingness to engage with suppliers clogs the whole innovation chain for the industry, preventing their sales group from achieving any differentiation.

An example of a co-creative, multi-party partnership can be found in the packaging industry where a company called Spear, a small family firm, recently acquired by the Austrian packaging group Constantia,[8] has successfully orchestrated a rich stream of innovation in a traditional industry: the development, manufacture and application of beer labels.[9] Two technological developments that have occurred over the last ten years are particularly noteworthy, and can be credited to Spear and the co-creative system it has quarterbacked. First, the traditional paper-based, glue and stick label found on beer bottles (e.g., old-fashioned Budweiser label) is being increasingly replaced by transparent, plastic-based pressure-sensitive adhesives labels (e.g., Bud Light bottles), which offer greater possibilities to make the beer stand out on the shelf as compared to the traditional paper label. Second, the new plastic-based, transparent labels can be removed from the bottles at regular wash temperatures, making those bottles fully recyclable in spite of the presence of solvents in the adhesives, and allowing the beer companies to become more sustainable (the adhesive cleanly stays with the label that gets removed).

Spear is, in the jargon of the industry, a "converter", which means they print the beer labels at high speed on huge rolls of plastic films they purchase from suppliers, cut the rolls to length and width (there are multiple pictures of the beer label across those large rolls) and deliver those narrow, shorter films to the packaging lines of large, global beer companies. Most importantly—and herein lies their co-creative role—they are the point of convergence between their suppliers' innovation in materials design and production efficiency, and their customers' endless quest for packaging speed and marketing creativity.

On the supply side, their procurement group works particularly closely with Avery Dennison, a $6.3 billion supplier company best known for its pressure-sensitive adhesives products.[10] Avery Dennison is a highly profitable company and produced a remarkable 18.3% return on average equity in 2014. Spear engages more specifically with Avery-Dennison's Fasson Division,

[8] For a description of the acquisition of Spear by Constantia, see article in Labels and Labeling magazine at http://www.labelsandlabeling.com/news/installations/constantia-flexibles-completes-acquisition-spear-group.
[9] For an illustration of Spear's creativity in designing beer labels, see 2012 article in Labels and Labeling entitled Spear provides labels for new beer brand, available at http://www.labelsandlabeling.com/news/labelexposure/spear-provides-labels-new-beer-brand.
[10] See Avery Dennison 2014 annual report, available at http://www.investors.averydennison.com/phoenix.zhtml?c=97892&p=irol-irhome.

which develops, manufactures and sells jumbo rolls of adhesive-coated plastic film that Spear prints on with the name of your favorite brew. Fasson's business involves running large process plants that manufacture laminate rolls made of a plastic film they buy, some adhesives they develop in their R&D department (pressure-sensitive adhesives are one of the two core know-hows of Avery-Dennison), and a paper liner that will be removed at the time of application to the beer bottle. Fasson's second key know-how lies in the ability to industrialize the manufacturing of the laminate films: its production lines are huge (both wide and long) and run continuously at extremely high speed to achieve the lowest possible cost.

On the sales side, Spear's customers are the procurement department of large global brewers. They have a particularly close relationship with Anheuser Bush InBev, which had sales of $47.1 billion in 2014 and an eye-popping EBITDA margin of 39% that same year.[11] Anheuser-Bush InBev pioneered with Spear and Fasson the first application of pressure-sensitive, plastic-based labels on beer bottles with the launch of its new Bud Light product many years ago, giving the bottle its original cool-looking, transparent blue light look.[12] Since then, the companies have developed a complete array of groundbreaking labels targeted, more and more, to specific populations.

The Spear's account executive at Anheuser Bush InBev is continuously challenged to solve several issues. First, Anheuser Bush InBev wants the label to be highly visual and attractive since it is an integral part of the company's marketing communication. The more complex the design, the harder it is to manufacture on the printing presses of Spear. The procurement staff of Spear responsible for sourcing materials from the Fasson Division of Avery Dennison works in close partnership with the Anheuser Bush InBev account manager, because they participate in the same co-creative system. Achieving high productivity for both Anheuser-Bush InBev and Spear is highly dependent on how the laminate designed and manufactured by Fasson will behave down the production chain. Spear is a master at creating insights from integrating the large and diverse amount of data to be taken into consideration

[11] See Anheuser Bush InBev 2014 annual report, available at http://www.ab-inbev.com/content/dam/universaltemplate/abinbev/pdf/media/annual-report/ABInBev_AR_14_EN_Financials.pdf.
[12] See 2004 article in Packaging World entitled Bud Light Goes to No-Label Look, available at http://www.packworld.com/package-component/films/bud-light-goes-no-label-look.

in optimizing the design and production process of the beer label value chain across Fasson Avery Dennison, Spear, and Anheuser Bush. Spear has developed proprietary technical tools that help visualize the label on the label, derive its specifications for printing and slitting, and laminate fabrication, and compute the total cost of ownership of various label designs on various machines. The company shares some of this data with its supplier, customer and equipment partner, but has to protect itself at all times from a potential squeeze play between its powerful material supplier and its giant beer customers.

Being a beer company sales account manager at Spear is a demanding task, because it requires organizing problem-solving sessions between R&D, engineering, quality, sales and procurement people across three different companies. It requires fostering the development and use of data-driven tools that continuously enrich the design of label products and label operations across the complex design and manufacturing chain involved. Ultimately, the Spear account manager is placed in a favorable negotiation position where he no longer solely competes on price. Similarly, the buyers at Anheuser-Bush InBev and Spear participate in the value-creating process above and beyond the traditional price negotiation role of commodity buyers.

Much remains to be done in extending co-creation beyond a supplier and customer. There are increasingly more readily available technology platforms that facilitate a multi-party exchange of data and insights in R&D, supply chain management, or even lifecycle management of products and services. The main barrier is now an organizational and cultural one, making the development of new skills in sales and procurement particularly urgent.

5   Level Five: Organize and Transform an Entire Ecosystem

The fifth and deepest level of co-creation involves organizing or transforming an entire ecosystem. It is the rarest form of co-creation today, but the rapid development of technologies, such as sensors and the Internet of Things, and the need to solve large industry-wide, or societal problems, are rapidly forcing companies to look at ecosystem co-creation as their strategy. At this highest level of co-creation, senior procurement people have to become orchestrators of the entire upstream chain, making the industry supply chain more transparent and data-rich. Strategic account managers can do the same with their downstream supply chains, offering transparency and insights that foster the development of new business opportunities beyond their immediate customers' procurement, or even their customers' customers.

The formation of new ecosystems, or the transformation of existing ecosystems, often (but not always) involve capitalizing on the broad mobilizing power of societal problems, such as climate change, sustainability, poverty, inequality, health, human rights or individual freedom issues. As long as each link in the chain is analyzed individually, these problems cannot be solved. When a few companies' procurement or sales leaders start orchestrating the ecosystem, they can sometimes move an entire industry in a different direction.

Unilever offers a case in point with its sustainability program. Unilever had revenues of €48.4 billion in 2014 and a staggering return on equity of 34.9%,[13] with iconic brands such as Dove, Lipton, Axe or Ben & Jerry's. The Unilever sustainability program—called Compass—involves all brands and global regions of Unilever and constitutes the cornerstone of the entire company's strategy. We focus, more specifically, on the company's orchestration of a new tomato ecosystem. Tomatoes are a key ingredient in products, such as Knorr soup, one of the main brands of Unilever. Unilever estimates that it buys about 3% of the global processed tomato production[14] and is one of the leaders in the transformation of the tomato agriculture-food value chain toward sustainability.

The agricultural chain for tomatoes is a long one. It is made of individual farmers who work for large tomato production processing groups such as Agraz in Spain, Cofco in China, or Morningstar in the US, who, in turn sell to Knorr, a division of Unilever. Achieving the costs and environmental standards demanded by Knorr requires that seed producers (such as Syngenta), pesticide manufacturers, such as BASF, or again, Syngenta, and agricultural equipment manufacturers, such as Deere, also participate in the development of new agricultural practices that are then implemented by the farmers. But the chain also extends downstream beyond Unilever to the large grocery stores such, as Carrefour, Tesco or Walmart where Knorr products are sold; these retailers have their own cost and sustainability standards. How does one

[13] See Unilever 2014 annual report, available at https://www.unilever.com/Images/ir_unilever_ar14_tcm244-421557_en.pdf. Authors' computation for return on equity.
[14] Source: Sustainable Sourcing section of the company website at http://www.unilever-foodsolutions.ie/sustainable-living/sustainable-sourcing.

go about transforming this entire value chain, from an industrially-driven, cost-only model to one where productivity and sustainability come together?

The first Unilever answer is an organizational one: the sustainability role has been entrusted to its Chief Purchasing Officer for Ingredients, which includes tomatoes. Rather than have a functional Chief Sustainability Office who tries to influence the line procurement person from the sidelines, as in many other organizations, the CPO owns both the procurement and the sustainability function. If you're a tomato supplier, you understand that both are part of your scorecard, and are on an equal footing, which removes the classic "do you want it sustainable or do you want it cheap" trade-off. The Unilever tomato sourcing function is where the buck stops for the entire chain.

The other weapon of Unilever is the use of a supply-chain-wide platform, called Quickfire,[15] which allows tomato producers along the chain to perform a self-assessment of where they stand against the Unilever 11-point sustainability program and communicate this position to Unilever. Unilever utilizes the data to evaluate the supplier, but also to pinpoint where more effort is needed, and Unilever frequently engages in joint efforts with its suppliers as opposed to simply keeping score. The Ingredients Chief Purchasing Officer is both the sheriff and the orchestrator of the global processed tomato value chain and regularly launches and manages global initiatives aimed at improving the tomato value chain. Coached by Unilever, suppliers all along the Knorr tomato chain are slowly learning to co-create and generate new innovative practices as a group.

We will likely see more and more ecosystem development, or transformation driven by large societal imperatives in the future, often involving complex systems of private sector companies working together, and often extending into public-private partnerships. As is already true for Unilever's purchasing function, the skills required of strategic account managers and procurement people will change dramatically as they are asked to drive the implementation of such broad ecosystem strategies, extending both the perimeter of responsibility beyond their firm and their immediate customer or supplier, but also the functional skills they are asked to master in terms of strategy, policy, social or sustainability skills.

---

[15] For a description of Quickfire technology, see Muddy Boots website at http://en.muddyboots.com/casestudy/view/driving-sustainability-agenda-with-suppliers.

In this final chapter, we have tried to illustrate the five levels at which senior sales and procurement people inside B2B businesses can co-create, from simple mobilization of their buying and selling networks all the way to organizing or transforming entire ecosystems. While not all companies will require that their SAMs or senior procurement people reach all the way to level five, most of them will require that both functions get on the journey.

Printed in the United States of America